MW00773460

First edition

Paperback ISBN: 979-8-9871373-4-5

Kindle ISBN: 979-8-9871373-5-2

Erase the Penalty

A Tax Professional's Guide to Abatement

Robert Nordlander, CPA
C. Steven Boon, EA

Former IRS Agents

Nordlander CPA, PLLC

Nordlander CPA, PLLC

To our families who make all things possible.

To all the current and former IRS employees who mentored us and dedicated themselves to making it a better place for all.

Contents

1. Introduction   1

2. Disclosure of Tax Information   6

3. Types of IRS Penalties   20

4. International Penalties   36

5. Grounds for Abatement   41

6. Failure to File / Failure to Pay   66

7. Failure to Pay Estimated Taxes   74

8. Accuracy-Related Penalties   83

9. Tax Return Preparer Penalties   87

10. Important Documentation   90

11. IRS Abatement Procedures   94

12. Reasonable Cause Assistant   105

13. State Penalty Abatement   116

14. Former IRS Employee Interviews   120

15. Conclusion   130

Epilogue   132

Appendix   133

About the authors

Robert Nordlander is a CPA, speaker, educator, author, podcast host, and nationally recognized expert in forensic accounting, criminal tax defense, and tax resolution. He is a retired special agent with IRS-Criminal Investigation. For over 20 years he found, evaluated, investigated, and prosecuted tax and money laundering crimes. The IRS also sent him to teach overseas to foreign law enforcement on how to investigate tax and money laundering crimes. Prior to his law enforcement career, he practiced in public accounting and taught various accounting and tax courses at a university. He is currently the sole shareholder of Nordlander CPA, PLLC, a boutique forensic accounting and tax resolution firm located in North Carolina. His forensic accounting and tax resolution courses are found nationwide on various education platforms. He has an Bachelor of Science degree in accounting, and a MBA from the University of North Carolina at Greensboro. Robert is a fan of the writings of J.R.R Tolkien and C.S. Lewis, and finishes long distance runs, albeit at the back of the pack.

C. Steven Boon is an Enrolled Agent based in the Greensboro-area of North Carolina. His firm, Boon Tax Resolution LLC, specializes in resolving IRS disputes. He holds a Bachelor of Science degree in accounting as well as an MBA from the University of Tennessee at Chattanooga. He is a former special agent with IRS-Criminal Investigation with nearly two decades of experience in income tax cases. In Criminal Investigation, Steven had a wide range of experiences working with the various IRS operating divisions, which he credits for giving him insight into the agency's inner workings and workplace culture. Today, he leverages this knowledge to help his clients navigate their tax issues effectively. Outside of work, Steven enjoys spending time with his family, pursuing his fitness goals, and volunteering his time ministering to senior adults in an assisted living center.

Chapter One

Introduction

Y ou have experienced it firsthand, perhaps on more occasions than you care to admit. A client walks into your office carrying paperwork and displaying an apprehensive expression. They have received letters from the IRS, and in their box of documents you see many of the envelopes are unopened. It's a common occurrence for taxpayers to not open their IRS correspondence. For them, those letters are too important to throw away, but too scary to open. Those clients want you to be braver than them. The fear of opening an envelope and deciphering what the IRS wants is the same as a claustrophobic client's fear of exploring a cave. Contained in those notices are almost guaranteed to be additional taxes, and for sure, penalties, all written in a language that is hard to understand. In 2021, the IRS assessed almost 41 million penalties totaling over $37 billion.[1] As a tax professional, you are hired to help them with their tax compliance. Part of that compliance is knowing how to remove penalties, if feasible,

---

1. Internal Revenue Service, U.S. Dep't of Treasury, Data Book, pg. 61 (2021).

that the IRS quickly and, possibly, prematurely assessed. As standard procedure, the IRS will assess penalties first and never consider that they could be wrong in their assumptions. Let's face it: getting penalized by the IRS can be more than just an annoyance; it can be a disaster. Unpaid taxes, in addition to the high penalties, can quickly develop into liens, levies, and even criminal charges if the matter is unresolved. This is not an exaggeration; rather, it is a reality that many people must deal with frequently due to basic ignorance or the failure to follow instructions.

This book is to help tax professionals like you learn the maze of penalty abatement. And as an enrolled agent, certified public accountant, or tax lawyer, you know too well that these penalties can be crippling, especially if the taxpayer has ignored the IRS for years.

Why are we concentrating on IRS penalties? Because they are not merely an annoyance, but rather a substantial obstruction to getting the IRS off a taxpayer's back. A previously manageable tax burden can become a financial catastrophe when penalties increase the tax due rapidly. You know the snowball effect consists of penalties for failing to file, late payments, and various other penalties the IRS deems to be appropriate punishments. What may have begun as an innocuous oversight has the potential to escalate into a situation that threatens the financial viability of your client.

But all is not lost when penalties are assessed. You do have some control over the circumstance and can take action. Whether you need assistance with penalties associated with a delinquent tax return or from a lack of due diligence, options are available. In public accounting and tax preparation businesses, you see penalties often.

Knowing and understanding the intricacies of the IRS pays huge dividends in your tax practice. Imagine how satisfying it would be to tell a client that you have not only fixed the tax problems they are currently facing but also abated the penalties. Imagine their happiness, their appreciation, and yes, even their recommendations. Your knowledge becomes more than simply a service; it's a necessity.

In this book, be prepared to interpret IRS jargon in an applicable and actionable manner and to be tutored by former IRS employees who were responsible for evaluating abatement requests. By the end of this book, you will not only be able to navigate the complexity of IRS penalties, but you will also know how to turn a client's despair into a sigh of relief. Both will be in your arsenal to fight back for your client. Regarding IRS penalties, ignorance is not a luxury and can be quite costly.

Therefore, let's begin with "Erase the Penalty." This excursion aims to provide you with the tools necessary to transform those annoying IRS penalties from a detested mark into a resolved issue.

This book will equip you with the strategies to confront various IRS penalties head-on. You will acquire an in-depth comprehension of the "reasonable cause" standards utilized by the IRS and the most effective means of utilizing this knowledge. You will learn about the First-Time Penalty Abatement Waiver, an often-overlooked but powerful weapon in your arsenal.

You will learn how to negotiate the confusing maze of IRS regulations and procedures, file for penalty abatement, and establish a compelling case for reasonable cause. As a bonus, in the appendix at the end of the book, you will read exactly the software questions and answers that IRS employees use to evaluate your penalty abatement request.

This book is your advanced course, your guide to turning the complicated world of IRS penalties into a terrain you can easily explore. It is not only about theory but also about insights that can be put into practice. "Erase the Penalty" prepares you for success in various areas, including deciphering IRS language and comprehending the appeals procedure.

This book's scope is intended to be thorough, covering most of what you will see in your tax practice. We will discuss the various forms of penalties, ranging from simple delinquent tax returns to fraudulent deductions. However, it is not merely a list; rather, each penalty is broken down into intelligible bits and studied to uncover what causes it and what may be able to reverse it.

We will include policies about reductions for first-time offenders and explanations of reasonable cause. We will walk you through each potential reason for IRS to consider to provide a comprehensive understanding of how these factors can come into play in real-world circumstances. These are not merely academic exercises; the answers are court rulings in the real world meant to prepare you for consultations with clients.

The purpose of this book is to position you as the go-to authority on penalty relief by ensuring you are familiar with the topic's "why" and "how." The purpose of this book is to provide you with a toolkit, which consists of a collection of techniques, action steps, and resources that may be directly applied in your practice. You'll want to keep this guide close, especially for the next anxious client who walks through your door, because it contains much useful information.

One of the enjoyable parts of tax resolution is analyzing what the IRS has done and knowing how to fix it or how to create a compelling argument to get relief for the client. Imagine looking your customers straight in the eye and confidently reassuring them that you have options to investigate, methods to implement, and a solid plan to deal with the consequences they face. This is the kind of benefit "Erase the Penalty" offers for your training routine.

You are not just adding another skill to your repertoire as you embark on the trip through the pages of this book; rather, you are becoming a lifeline for your clients and a beacon of hope in a system that frequently feels merciless.

Legal Disclaimer

An effort has been made to write a book about penalty abatement that is true and accurate. The abatement of most penalties is an art and not a science. There may be more than one way to get a penalty removed. And not all IRS employees reviewing penalty abatement requests will agree on the final outcome of the abatement given the same set of facts. This book is not an all-encompassing treatise on penalty abatement. This book is meant to give you the best possible chance of getting a penalty abated. There are no guarantees in dealing with the IRS. Every taxpayer and circumstance is slightly different. Most taxpayer problems are the same, but there are a few outliers. So please remember that tax laws change and policies change. I hope this book serves you well in helping your clients with their IRS penalties.

Chapter Two

Disclosure of Tax Information

The IRS is very serious about keeping tax return and tax information secret. No one wants to be known as or accused of being a tax cheat or rumored to be having financial problems. The tax system of the United States requires the taxpayer to voluntarily turn over their personal financial information. If not turned over voluntarily, then the IRS has the tools needed to involuntarily get that information, but the onus is on the taxpayer first. I believe that most people are more comfortable being naked in public than sharing with the public their personal financial information. The IRS receives financial information from taxpayers and other sources, and it can't share any tax information without legal authority.

The United States Congress established rules and regulations regarding the disclosure of tax information, which are codified at I.R.C. § 6103. I.R.C. is shorthand for the tax code (aka Internal Revenue Code).

There are civil and criminal penalties for the government employee violating this section. In 2023, an IRS contractor was prosecuted with disclosing the tax return information of very wealthy taxpayers to the media.[1] That is why the IRS employees take this section very seriously; there are civil and criminal consequences for their actions. In general, when the IRS receives tax returns and tax return information, it becomes a one-way street, whereby they keep that information secret and don't disclose it easily to others, even to other government agencies. There are rules governing disclosing various information that the IRS receives. Section 6103 ensures that the nosy neighbor, jealous ex-lover, and the suspicious mother-in-law cannot demand your tax information held by the IRS. The information is held in secret unless an exception is listed in section 6103.

Generally, tax information held by the IRS is in two categories: tax return and return information. The disclosure laws have defined the differences. If someone conducts research on what tax information can be disclosed, just remember that the policies and laws are written with these terms in mind. If you see these terms in government documents, it is easy to gloss over them, thinking it covers ALL information, which it does not. And don't feel bad if things get confusing. Even the most veteran IRS employee at times gets confused.

Per the IRS guidelines, a return is defined as:

---

1. Press Release, U.S. Dep't of Justice, IRS Contractor Pleads Guilty to Disclosing Tax Return Information to News Organizations (October 12, 2023), *available at* https://www.justice.gov/opa/pr/irs-contractor-pleads-guilty -disclosing-tax-return-information-news-organizations .

Any tax or information return, declaration of estimated tax, or claim for refund required by, or provided for or permitted under, the provisions of the Code which is filed with the Secretary by, on behalf of, or with respect to any person, and any amendment or supplement thereto, including supporting schedules, attachments, or lists which are supplemental to, or part of, the return so filed.[2]

In the same section, return information is defined as including:

... a taxpayer's identity, the nature, source, or amount of income, payments, receipts, deductions, exemptions, credits, assets, liabilities, net worth, tax liability, tax withheld, deficiencies, overassessments, or tax payments; whether the taxpayer's return is subject to collection, examination, investigation, or any other actions taken by the Secretary with respect to federal filing requirements.[3]

By default, the IRS cannot simply disclose any information to anyone for any reason. However, as with most laws, there are exceptions. If there is a request for tax information to the IRS, the request

---

2. Internal Revenue Service, U.S. Dep't of Treasury, Internal Revenue Manual § 4.2.5.1.4 (2022), *available at* https://www.irs.gov/irm/part4/irm_04-002-005r.

3. *Id.*

must fit into the category of exceptions listed in section 6103. For tax professionals, there are three main exceptions permitting the IRS to disclose tax information: when the request comes from the taxpayer, the taxpayer's representative, or a person with a "material interest."

Internal Revenue Manual

While the tax code allows the disclosure, there's also a handbook for IRS employees to use when implementing the law that shows the IRS interpretation of the tax code. The Internal Revenue Manual (IRM) is a public document that is the handbook for IRS employees when making decisions and implementing policy. The IRM is organized by sections and subsections. For example, IRM chapter 9 is about criminal tax investigations and IRM chapter 25 discusses summonses. The IRM can be easily accessed through an internet search engine.

Code of Federal Regulations

Another important document to know is the Code of Federal Regulations (C.F.R.). It consists of the rules published by government agencies and departments. Typically, the C.F.R. section number mimics that of the related statute. I.R.C. § 6103(c) may allow the IRS to disclose tax information, and 26 C.F.R. § 301.6103(c)[4] gives more detail regarding what the IRS requires to get the information. Section 6103 is in both the I.R.C. and C.F.R. If you know the I.R.C. statute number, then the implementation of it will be the same number in the C.F.R. Many times, the United States Congress allows agencies,

---

4. Treas. Reg. § 301.6103(c)-1 (as amended in 2013).

such as the IRS, to create regulations related to their agencies. This makes sense when you think about it. The United States Congress isn't interested in creating laws regarding where to file a tax return. The IRS is given the authority to administer the tax law, including to designate the location for the tax return to be sent. This power also comes with a downside: in implementing its tax functions, the IRS can create unreasonable expectations with the stroke of a pen.

Disclosing Tax Information to the Taxpayer

I.R.C. § 6103(e) allows the taxpayer access to his/her return and return information. When a taxpayer wants information about what was reported to the IRS or what was filed, etc., then the taxpayer is allowed access to that information. Information also can include open examinations of the taxpayer's tax liabilities. This isn't a blanket disclosure though. If the United States Treasury believes that anything in the taxpayer's file can "seriously impair" an investigation, then the information can be withheld. Such impairment could be from a whistle blower's allegation, law enforcement undercover operations, etc.

Disclosing Tax Information with "Material Interest"

I.R.C. § 6103(e) also allows for information to be disclosed to individuals having a "material interest." This allows disclosure to individuals who are involved in partnerships or have an interest in a business. A partner should be allowed access to certain tax information related to the partnership. The same is true with corporations, but the individual must be a corporate officer, an employee who is authorized to access tax information, or a taxpayer owning at least 1% of the voting stock. Other individuals who can access information include bankruptcy trustees, administrators of an estate or trust, and certain beneficiaries of an estate or trust.

Disclosing Tax Information to a Designee

I.R.C. § 6103(c) allows information to be disclosed to the taxpayer's designee. Many times, the taxpayer who has the right to the tax information held by the IRS wants to disclose this information to another person. The taxpayer's designee can be anyone, such as a bank, tax adviser, law enforcement, etc. The return and return information can be disclosed to the taxpayer's designee unless the disclosure would "seriously impair" an investigation.

However, if the designee is to act on the taxpayer's behalf as their representative, then certain qualifications must exist. A qualified representative cannot be any person from the general public; in general, the representative must be a CPA, EA, or attorney. As a qualified professional, the IRS created Circular 230 which are the rules and regulations governing representatives when representing taxpayers to the IRS. Every tax professional should read Circular 230, because violating those regulations allows the IRS to issue penalties and exclude them from IRS tax representation. Such rules include the representative failing to file a tax return, which can result in the IRS revoking the tax representative's ability to practice before the IRS.[5]

Here are some of the highlights regarding disclosure of information that are listed in the IRM:

---

5. Treasury Department Circular No. 230, § 10.51(6) (Rev. 6-2014)

What Forms Allow Disclosure?

IRM 4.2.5.4[6] gives guidance on what forms are used to authorize disclosure:

- I.R.C. § 6103(c) and 26 C.F.R. § 301.6103(c)-1 allow the IRS to make disclosures of federal tax returns or return information to persons or organizations designated by the taxpayer.[7]

- The IRS typically requires a Form 2848 (Power of Attorney) or Form 8821 (Tax Information Authorization) as proper authorization to disclose tax matters to attorneys-in-fact or designees.

- Form 4506-T (Request for Transcript of Tax Return) is available for disclosure of only transcripts of tax returns to designees and is commonly used to allow banks access to only the tax return, thus limiting access to other tax information.

- Form 56 (Notice Concerning Fiduciary Relationship) is used to show the existence of a fiduciary relationship. A fiduciary (trustee, executor, administrator, receiver, or guardian) stands in the position of a taxpayer and acts as the taxpayer, not as a representative. A fiduciary can hire a representative

---

6. Internal Revenue Service, U.S. Dep't of Treasury, Internal Revenue Manual § 4.2.5.4 (2022), *available at* https://www.irs.gov/irm/part4/irm_04-002-005r.

7. I.R.C. § 6103(c) (2024); Treas. Reg. § 301.6103(c)-1 (as amended in 2013).

(CPA, EA, or attorney) to act on behalf of the person or entity by filing the Form 2848. The fiduciary must sign the power of attorney on behalf of the person or entity.

- Disclosure authority is limited to only those tax years and the type of tax listed on the authorization forms.

What Information Is Available?

IRM 4.2.5.6[8] states that taxpayers have the right to information, unless it is protected by privilege:

- Taxpayers have a right to receive their return information (administrative file and workpapers) unless it would impair the tax administration.

- The administrative file and workpapers may contain pre-decisional draft documents and the thoughts and impressions of IRS counsel or employees. Such materials might need to be redacted under the deliberative process privilege, the attorney-client privilege, or the attorney work product doctrine.

---

8. Internal Revenue Service, U.S. Dep't of Treasury, Internal Revenue Manual § 4.2.5.6 (2022), *available at* https://www.irs.gov /irm/part4/irm_04-002-005r.

What if Spouses Have Joint Tax Returns?

Sometimes, there is a need to gather information regarding a spouse, but the spouses are separated and no longer living together. But what happens if there is a joint liability, and now the spouses are not talking to one another?

IRM 4.2.5.8[9] gives guidance regarding what can be disclosed during a marital conflict:

- In cases of individual taxpayers who filed joint returns, I .R.C. § 6103(e)(8) authorizes the IRS to disclose certain information to taxpayers or their authorized representatives regarding efforts to collect a joint tax liability from the other individual.

- The IRS may disclose limited information related to the collection of the joint tax liability from the other individual.

- More guidance is available in IRM 11.3.2.4.1.1 (Disclosure of Collection Activities with Respect to Joint Returns).[10]

One spouse doesn't have automatic access to IRS records regarding another spouse. Their joint tax return is open for each person's inspection, but the income, assets, etc. relating to the spouse are not.

---

9. Internal Revenue Service, U.S. Dep't of Treasury, Internal Revenue Manual § 4.2.5.8 (2022), *available at* https://www.irs.gov/irm/part4/irm_04-002-005r.

10. Internal Revenue Service, U.S. Dep't of Treasury, Internal Revenue Manual § 11.3.2.4.1.1 (2020), *available at* https://www.irs.gov/irm/part11/irm_11-003-002.

For example, the wages reported on a joint tax return can be disclosed, but the wages earned (as reported by the employer to the IRS) cannot.

Interestingly, the use of a dependent's information by a taxpayer is not an exception. It's not uncommon to see a dependent's information being unlawfully used on someone else's tax return. In filing tax returns with dependents, the first tax return that claims a dependent will be accepted by the IRS. Later, when another tax return claims the same dependent, the second tax return will be rejected by the IRS, with an explanation that the dependent was already used. This causes a problem especially when someone takes the dependent's information and gets a larger refund, but then a parent later rightfully uses the dependent's information and that tax return gets rejected. Of course, the parent calls the IRS, and the IRS states that the dependent was already used. When the parent asks whose return it was claimed on, the IRS refuses to turn over that information, leaving the parent to file a complaint with the IRS to dispute the dependent status. As expected, the rightful parent will wait a long time for the IRS to issue the refund.

Tax Information Is Kept on Transcripts

When you attended high school or college, you received a copy of your transcript to prove your education. The school transcript showed the courses taken, the number of credits earned, the grade in each course, and the grade point average. The IRS is no different with their record keeping. The IRS keeps records of a taxpayer's account (individual or business), which is shown on a transcript. There are various "transcripts" kept by the IRS. The transcripts are known by the command codes used in the computer. This goes back to the early days of MS-DOS in the 1980s. A person would physically type a command into the computer to access information. Even if the IRS updates its software, the method and lingo for the IRS goes back to those early years. If you ask for a complete transcript, that is also known as a MFTRA-C. The IRS employee will use a command code in the computer for MFTRA-C. So, depending on what information you are looking for, you will require a different transcript. If you ask an IRS employee for a transcript, you will need to explain in detail what you are asking for, or if necessary, use their shorthand by giving the command code.

Here are the main types of transcripts that are accessible to the public via the online portal at IRS.gov:

- Tax Return Transcript - shows most line items from the original Form 1040-series tax return as filed, along with any forms and schedules. It doesn't show changes made after the original tax return was filed. This transcript is available for the current and three prior tax years. A tax return transcript usually meets the needs of lending institutions offering mortgages and student loans. This shows business tax returns as well.

- Tax Account Transcript - shows basic data such as filing status, taxable income, and payment types. It also shows activities made after the original return was filed, such as tax payments, penalties, etc.

- Record of Account Transcript - combines the tax return and tax account transcripts above into one complete transcript. This transcript is available for the current and three prior tax years using Get Transcript Online or Form 4506-T.

- Wage and Income Transcript - shows data from information returns the IRS received such as Forms W-2, 1098, 1099, and 5498. The message, "No record of return filed" for the current tax year means that third-party information has not populated to the transcript yet. It usually updates between late May and July for the previous year's data. So, the 2021 Form W-2 information sent from an employer won't be posted in the IRS database until spring of 2022. This transcript is available for the current and nine prior tax years using Get Transcript Online or Form 4506-T.

Reading the Transcripts

Tax account transcripts are organized by SSN/EIN, year, and the type of tax. Even though they share the same EIN, business income tax returns won't be confused with payroll tax returns for the same year. Every tax and period stands on its own.

The type of tax is defined by Master File Tax Account Code (MFT). Payroll taxes are MFT 01; personal income tax returns are MFT 30. When reviewing a transcript, the transcript is in chronological order with the most recent year at the beginning of the transcript. Here is a summary of the most common MFT codes:

MFT Code	Form	Description
01	941	Employer's Quarterly Federal Tax Return
02	1120	US Corporate Income Tax Return
05	1041	US Income Tax Return for Estates & Trusts
06	1065	US Return of Partnership Income
10	940	Employer's Annual Federal Unemployment (FUTA) Tax Return
30	1040	US Individual Income Tax Return
31	1040	Assessments against person on a joint return i.e., bankruptcy, OIC, Innocent Spouse
55	1040	Trust Fund Recovery Penalty

Most of the transcripts are not English-friendly, but show transaction codes, meaning that you will need to look up the code to determine what occurred. In a typical transcript, the type of return, period, date of the activity, and transaction code will be shown. For example, when the IRS receives a Form 1040, a transaction code 150 will be shown with a date. This means that the IRS received a Form 1040 on that date. Different transaction codes will be shown for penalties, interest, additional taxes, referral of the tax return to collection, etc. Without an understanding of what the codes mean, the reader will not understand the actions taken by the IRS. It takes practice to understand what these codes mean.

Other transcripts that, internally, IRS employees use quite often and will require a specific request:

1. MFTRA - a full transcript showing the various transactions associated with the account, including notices that were mailed to the taxpayer.

2. IRPTRL - a listing of third-party data that was filed with the IRS, such as dividend income, mortgage interest, wages, interest income, pension income, social security income, etc. This transcript is all inclusive, including when banks file currency transaction reports. Based on my experience, the IRPTRL has more information than the Wage and Income Transcript.

3. IMFOLI - a listing of tax due per period associated with the various tax forms, such as Form 941, Form 1120, etc. This gives a quick summary of what type of taxes are due and for what time period.

4. TAXMODA - used by revenue officers (RO) because it shows the collection status expiration date (CSED), which is the date that collections must cease

Various software companies that specialize in deciphering IRS transcripts can assist in translating the IRS transaction codes to plain, understandable English.

Summary

In summary, the IRS doesn't disclose tax information unless authorized by I.R.C. § 6103. Authorization by the taxpayer to disclose information is on two main forms: Form 2848 (Power of Attorney) or Form 8821 (Tax Information Authorization). Form 4506-T is commonly requested by banks to access only the taxpayer's filed tax return. Once the IRS receives proper authorization to disclose tax information, most of the relevant tax information is on transcripts. Depending on what information is being requested, a certain transcript is required. The most common transcripts are available through the online portal at www.irs.gov, but those transcripts won't be English friendly and will require deciphering, because the IRS uses transaction codes to describe activities.

Chapter Three

Types of IRS Penalties

N o one in their right mind likes penalties. In every sport imaginable, there are penalties for not abiding by the rules. For hockey, there's a penalty box. In soccer, there are yellow and red cards. And when the rules are broken, the referee or umpire announces a penalty and assesses the punishment to deter the bad behavior. At times, a unique problem will exist which requires the sport's ruling authority to add new rules to the current rulebook, so they create additional penalties to stop what they deem inappropriate. The United States Congress and the IRS are no different. Some problems are unforeseen for years, and then a new penalty is created to solve the problem. Unfortunately, like in sports, the types of penalties available to the IRS for taxpayers keeps increasing. In 1955, there were approximately 14 penalties in the Internal Revenue Code. Now there are 10 times that amount.[1]

According to IRM 20.1.1.2,[2] penalties have a purpose:

1. Penalties exist to encourage voluntary compliance by supporting the standards of behavior required by the Internal Revenue Code.

2. For most taxpayers, voluntary compliance consists of preparing an accurate return, filing it timely, and paying any tax due. Efforts made to fulfill these obligations constitute compliant behavior. Most penalties apply to behavior that fails to meet any or all of these obligations.

With the ever-increasing arsenal of penalties, the United States Congress has authorized the IRS to review penalties that are deemed to be unfair to the taxpayer based on the circumstances. To treat taxpayers in a fair way, the IRS created a Penalty Handbook, which can be found in IRM 20.1.[3] This handbook contains the guidelines for IRS employees to hopefully administer fairly the penalties and

---

1. Internal Revenue Service, U.S. Dep't of Treasury, Internal Revenue Manual § 20.1.1.1.1 (2011), *available at* https://www.irs.gov/irm/part20/irm_20-001-001r.

2. Internal Revenue Service, U.S. Dep't of Treasury, Internal Revenue Manual § 20.1.1.2 (2017), *available at* https://www.irs.gov/irm/part20/irm_20-001-001r.

3. Internal Revenue Service, U.S. Dep't of Treasury, Internal Revenue Manual §§ 20.1 *et seq.* (2023), *available at* https://www.irs.gov/irm/part20.

the removal of penalties. Some penalties are automatic, which means that a computer generates the penalty without human intervention, such as failure to file a tax return or a failure to pay on time. The IRS computer knows that a tax return or payment is late, and subsequently issues a penalty notice. Other penalties such as a fraud penalty require a human being to assess the circumstances and determine if a penalty is warranted. In many cases, an IRS supervisor must sign off on the penalty that is recommended by an employee.[4]

When penalties are assessed to the taxpayer, the financial implications begin. As stated before, the IRS penalizes first and doesn't ask questions about its validity. Taxpayers on the receiving end suffer financially, of course. Not only do they owe the IRS (which isn't known for its kindness), but to fight the IRS requires hiring a tax professional, and any funds paying the IRS or the tax professional becomes an unknown opportunity cost to them. Money is finite, so if the IRS or tax professional gets the money, that is less money to invest for retirement, take a vacation, pay off that student loan, etc.

Emotional Cost of Penalties

Not only are there financial implications, but the emotional adds to the financial. Money, or the lack of it, carries an emotional element to it. Of course, the IRS knows this. That is why they implement these penalties to begin with. It's all about behavior, and to change behavior requires emotions. Depending on the type of penalty, such as the Trust Fund Recovery Penalty, the penalty can leap from a corporate problem to now a personal problem. And for those who are in relationships,

---

4. I.R.C. § 6751(b) (2022).

what affects one taxpayer is now going to affect many taxpayers. As a tax professional, the assessed penalties are probably a symptom of a larger problem, such as lack of record keeping, being prompt in responsibilities, integrity, etc. A true tax professional looks beyond the penalty and helps guide the taxpayer to change their behavior so that they don't get themselves in this problem again. That, of course, takes tact, empathy, and also "speaking the truth in love." When talking to taxpayers with tax problems, my role is to emphasize the underlying problem that caused the penalty to begin with, which may include recommending a new return preparer, new bookkeeping system, recording due dates on calendars, more oversight on the handling of payroll, and proper accounting to ensure cash flow to pay taxes timely.

Legal Consequences

Not only are there financial and emotional implications, but also potential legal consequences. When a taxpayer gets into IRS trouble and then the IRS piles on with penalties and interest, the IRS also starts adverse collection procedures, such as levying bank accounts, investment portfolios, and possible employment and business income. When this happens, the taxpayer believes that their only recourse is to hide assets and income from the IRS. The hiding of assets and income from the IRS is the leading cause of fraud referrals to IRS Criminal Investigation, the law enforcement arm of the IRS. IRS Criminal Investigation frequently receives referrals from its own agency about taxpayers evading the collection of taxes. When this happens, there's a high likelihood that your client may be going to prison for tax fraud, and you, the tax professional can expect to be interviewed by the IRS special agents and the federal prosecutors about what you know and the advice you gave to your client.

Even if IRS does not pursue criminal charges, the IRS has avenues to chase your client and continue to penalize if they think that other penalties regarding fraud are warranted.

Certain penalties are the aftermath of other questionable behavior, such as the fraud penalties. These types of penalties could become a stepping stone to professional licenses being revoked, particularly if the client is a tax professional. A significant tax penalty can cause the licensing board to reconsider the case, which might result in suspension or disbarment. This is a career derailment rather than merely a bump in the road. As the tax expert, you might be the only person preventing your client's professional destruction.

The legal repercussions of IRS penalties are not merely an additional layer of difficulty; they are an altogether separate animal. You are the first line of defense against a vast array of legal harm because you are the go-to tax expert. Your knowledge could mean the difference between a scenario that can be handled and a major legal issue. It's always a good idea to have other professionals, such as tax attorneys and criminal attorneys, in your contact list just in case your client needs additional assistance.

The whole picture for your client includes a difficult but crucial element: the emotional and psychological consequences of IRS penalties. Understanding these consequences can help you better customize your approach, demonstrate true empathy, and steer clear of the choppy emotional waters that IRS penalties can cause. Keep in mind that you are also managing lives, not simply numbers. And that alone makes a huge difference.

This chapter is to help you analyze the reasoning behind the various penalties and how each fits in the penalty abatement process. It is important to understand the underlying assumptions that the IRS is making to assess the penalty in the first place. Once you know the penalty and why it is assessed, you can seek out the specific abatement method. There are specific abatement methods, eligibility requirements, and justifications for each sort of penalty. Some penalties can be abated easily, while others may require a higher level of review or judicial finding. It really depends on the type of penalty.

Here are the most common types of penalties for both individuals, partnerships, and corporations. This is both for income tax returns and payroll tax returns:

- Failure to File - I.R.C. § 6651(a)(1)

- Failure to Pay - I.R.C. §§ 6651(a)(1) and (2)

- Failure to File Information Returns - I.R.C. § 6652

- Estimated Tax Penalty - I.R.C. § 6654

- Accuracy Related Penalty - I.R.C. § 6662

Failure-to-File and Failure-to-Pay Penalties

The two most common IRS penalties are failures to file and pay taxes. These two penalties are from the same statute: I.R.C. § 6651.

Let's start by discussing Failure-to-File. The name sums it up: your client failed to file a tax return by the deadline, typically April 15th for personal income tax returns. This penalty is particularly annoying because it increases quickly—5% of the unpaid tax per month, with a maximum of 25%. The catch is that if the return is over 60 days overdue, the minimum penalty is $435 or 100% of the unpaid tax, whichever is lower.

The Failure-to-Pay penalty will then follow behind the Failure to File penalty. Although a little less pushy, it accumulates at 0.5% of the unpaid monthly tax, with a 25% ceiling (ending 50 months later). The actual problem with this situation is the interest keeps compounding because the penalty continues to add to the tax bill for almost five years. What started out as a small debt, continues to increase over time because of this penalty, and then interest is also added.

To make it worse, both of these penalties may be imposed simultaneously. A client who doesn't file or pay on time risks being hit with two fines at once. Although the Failure-to-File penalty is typically more severe, the Failure-to-Pay penalty, of course, can continue for years.

Failure to File Certain Information Returns

If the tax return is for information purposes only and doesn't require a calculation of a tax due, the IRS still wants it filed timely. Such information returns can be Forms 990 for non-profits, Forms 1099 for reporting various income, Forms 1098 for various deductions, and Forms W-2 for employee wages. In 2023, the penalties can be steep as $50 per form (per payee) and increasing up to $290. For large employers, this can be a huge penalty when they fail to file forms such as the Forms W-2 on time. This penalty is most common for new accounting clerks who forget or when there is turnover in personnel. Because no tax is due with these returns, the IRS penalizes non-compliance by adding a penalty per form. I.R.C. § 6652 details what constitutes an information return.

Estimated Tax Penalty

One of the most complicated penalties is the failure to timely pay the proper estimated taxes. There are various rules and regulations that require an estimated tax payment and various exceptions to the rule. Typically, the estimated payment penalty is assessed on individuals who were either self-employed or own a business. Rarely is the estimated penalty assessed on a W-2 earning employee. Those employees earn wages and have no substantial income outside of their employment. Because its common occurrence is on self-employed individuals and business owners, the penalty abatement for the estimated tax penalty will be addressed in a separate chapter in this book.

Accuracy-Related Penalties

Accuracy-Related penalties are also available to the IRS under I.R.C. § 6662. When there is a "substantial understatement" of income tax or when the IRS finds that there has been carelessness or a disregard for laws and regulations, these penalties take effect. The typical penalty rate is 20% of the unpaid tax, but in more extreme circumstances, it can increase to 40%.

An understatement is generally considered "substantial" if it exceeds $5,000 or 10% of the actual tax. Complex forms with several earnings, deductions, and credits can make this a serious issue. One math error can upset the entire system.

These penalties can come from a smörgåsbord of circumstances that could affect the understatement of income taxes, which mostly centers around valuations. Such examples are

- Negligence toward or disregard of the rules or regulations

- Substantial understatement of income tax

- Substantial valuation misstatement

- Substantial estate or gift tax valuation understatement

- Gross valuation misstatement

- Undisclosed noneconomic substance transactions

- Undisclosed foreign financial asset understatement

- Inconsistent estate basis

More information on Accuracy-Related Penalties is located in IRM 20.1.5.[5]

Fraudulent Failure to File

If a taxpayer flatly refuses to file a tax return on time, the IRS has at its disposal I.R.C. 6651(f) which is the fraudulent failure to file. "Fraudulent" implies intentional wrongdoing—as opposed to an oversight or mistake. The IRS must demonstrate that your client purposefully failed to file their tax return to avoid paying taxes. As previously mentioned, there are already penalties that are assessed because of an error, but this penalty is when the taxpayer gets indignant with the government.

---

5. Internal Revenue Service, U.S. Dep't of Treasury, Internal Revenue Manual § 20.1.5 (2021), *available at* https://www.irs.gov/irm/part20/irm_20-001-005.

The fine for fraudulent failure to file is high: 15% of the tax owed per month, up to a maximum of 75%. You read that correctly: a penalty equal to 75% of the tax due may be applied. The consequences are the highest penalties available. As a side note, if your client qualifies for this penalty, he most likely qualifies for a criminal prosecution. Failure to file a tax return is a criminal violation as described in 26 U.S.C. § 7203.[6] I have seen these types of penalties on tax protesters, who refuse to acknowledge the legitimacy of the IRS or the tax code created by the United States Congress. In one example, a taxpayer was a W-2 employee but told his employer that he was exempt from federal withholdings, and then no federal income taxes were withheld from his paycheck for years. Of course, the employer filed the Form W-2 properly, so the IRS knew what the taxpayer's wages were. However, the taxpayer continued to misbehave to the point that the IRS created a substitute tax return, and later added penalties, to which the fraudulent failure to file applied.

Due to the severity of this penalty, the IRS typically only pursues this course of action after a careful examination. They don't haphazardly apply this penalty. If you find yourself handling a situation like this, you'll probably need to refer your client to a criminal tax defense attorney to mitigate any possible damage. This penalty can also be applied after a criminal tax investigation was completed.

Return Preparer Penalty

Many return preparers don't know this, but a return preparer can be penalized under I.R.C. § 6694 for understating a tax liability due

6. I.R.C. § 7203 (1990).

to an unreasonable position or willful/reckless conduct.[7] Common sense would dictate that a return preparer wouldn't engage in violating known tax laws for a client, but the penalty exists for a purpose. Some return preparers push the limits to absurdity. To qualify for this penalty, the return preparer knew (or reasonably should have known) that the position was unreasonable.

Frivolous Tax Submissions

Not to be forgotten are "Frivolous Tax Submissions." As a special agent with IRS-Criminal Investigation, I investigated a taxpayer who thought he could send the IRS a large bill demanding a large refund based on a crazy belief that the IRS was his debtor. After the IRS gave him official notice of the possible consequences of his frivolous filings, he continued his behavior by filing additional frivolous returns. The IRS finally ran out of patience for his crazy filings and assessed him a large penalty. A frivolous tax return, i.e., if your client files a tax return that is blatantly false or founded on a flimsy justification, is a $5,000 fine: for example, the claim that they are exempt from paying taxes because they disagree with how the government spends its money. Yes, it is possible to poke the bear with crazy unsubstantiated filings.

What makes these less well-known penalties important, then? Mostly that they can stack. A client may approach you with what first appears to be a simple Failure-to-Pay case, but upon closer inspection, you discover that they also have underpayment and information return penalties pending. Each of them has a unique set of guidelines

---

7. I.R.C. § 6694

and options for mitigation, making your position as the expert all the more crucial.

You will become a more adaptable tax expert, with the ability to handle a wider range of difficulties when you know these "curveball" penalties. Some of these penalties are frankly a warning sign that maybe a taxpayer is not worth having as a client. I recently saw a local tax lien for over $100,000 with some odd statutes listed. When I did some research on those penalty statutes, it was obvious that the taxpayer was self-employed, never filed a tax return, and filed frivolous filings for over a decade. I would personally decline dealing with these types of tax protesters. In my experience, once these people brainwash themselves into this corner, they don't come back to reality. They self-destruct themselves into either living in a cave fearing the end of the world, or in prison because they rejected a federal judge's authority.

Approval Prerequisite to Penalty Assessments

Most penalties require some type of human approval, but not all. Taxpayers have a right to know what penalty is assessed and the law that allows the IRS to assess it. In IRM 20.1.1.2.3,[8] it details the key points of I.R.C. § 6751(a) that requires that each penalty notice to include the name of the penalty, applicable I.R.C. section, and a computation of the penalty.

I.R.C. 6751(b)(1) states that in general, no penalty under the Internal Revenue Code shall be assessed unless the initial determination of

---

8. Internal Revenue Service, U.S. Dep't of Treasury, Internal Revenue Manual § 20.1.1.2.3 (2020), *available at* https://www.irs.gov/irm/part20/irm_20-001-001r.

such assessment is personally approved (in writing) by the immediate supervisor or higher of the individual making such determination. In 2023, the U.S. Tax Court issued a scathing report against the IRS because of potential backdating of the immediate supervisor's approval. The IRS claimed that the immediate supervisor's penalty approval was verbal, even though the signature was backdated. The Court didn't like that answer, but appeared to be more upset that once IRS lawyers discovered it, the Court wasn't notified immediately. The greatest takeaway from that ruling is that the Tax Court was not timely notified that the backdating occurred once the IRS discovered it. Supposedly the IRS has placed policies and controls to ensure that the backdating doesn't happen again.

The policy regarding the timing of supervisory approval can be found in IRM 20.1.1.2.3.1.[9]

For most penalties, the IRS notifies the taxpayer in the mail, which is the first time the taxpayer even knows that the IRS is upset. I.R.C. § 6751(b)(2) provides exceptions to the supervisory approval requirement for the following penalties, which are commonly issued by computer generated mass mailing. The following penalties don't require supervisor approval and you can expect them in a standardized computer generated letter:

1. I.R.C. § 6651, Failure to File Tax Return or to Pay Tax,

2. I.R.C. § 6654, Failure by Individual to Pay Estimated Income Tax,

---

9. Internal Revenue Service, U.S. Dep't of Treasury, Internal Revenue Manual § 20.1.1.2.3.1 (2020), *available at* https://www.irs.gov/irm/part20/irm_20-001-001r.

3. I.R.C. § 6655, Failure by Corporation to Pay Estimated Income Tax, and

4. Any penalties automatically calculated through electronic means. Penalties that are automatically calculated through electronic means are excluded from supervisory approval requirements. A penalty is only considered to be "automatically calculated through electronic means" if no human IRS employee makes an independent determination with respect to the applicability of the penalty.

Unless allowed by statute, the initial determination of the penalty must be personally approved in writing by the immediate supervisor, dated, and retained in the case file. Supervisory approval may be documented on a penalty approval form, in the form of an email, memo to file, or electronically. The approval must cover all tax years and penalties, including alternative penalties. This penalty approval should be maintained in the administrative file and used as the basis for the penalty assessment. This makes sense when you think about it. The taxpayer cannot be assessed a penalty until after the supervisor approves it, but there has to be a paper trail showing the penalty recommendation and the basis for it.

As a side note, accuracy-related penalties can be systemically assessed if the proposed penalty is sent to the taxpayer and the taxpayer doesn't contest the proposal. When ignored, the IRS can assess the penalty after 30 days. However, if the taxpayer contests the penalty, then the file must be reviewed by a human and a supervisor's approval will be needed before assessing the accuracy-related penalty. IRM 2

0.1.1.2.3.2 discusses the Automated Underreporter and Correspondence Examination Automation Support Programs.[10]

The penalties that you will often see will be computer generated without supervisor approval. However, on those penalties requiring supervisor approval, check the administrative file to ensure that it was properly documented. Never assume that the IRS employee has done their job adequately. I can tell you from experience that IRS employees do take shortcuts detrimental to the taxpayer's position.

Statute of Limitations on Abatement

Penalty abatements must be requested within a prescribed period of time. The normal refund statute expiration date (RSED) is three years from the date of the filed return or two years after the penalty was paid.[11] Therefore, keeping track of time is important because these refunds are guided by federal statute. More information on what constitutes as a timely request can be found in IRM 4.10.11.5.2.[12]

Summary

As you can see, there are many penalties that the IRS has at its disposal for administering the tax law. Most of these penalties are related to

---

10. Internal Revenue Service, U.S. Dep't of Treasury, Internal Revenue Manual § 20.1.1.2.3.2 (2020), *available at* https://www.irs.gov/irm/part20/irm_20-001-001r.

11. I.R.C. § 6511(a) and (b)

12. IRM 4.10.11.5.2

failure to timely pay taxes and the failure to timely file a tax return. Some penalties relate to bad behavior and not a mistake.

Because of its complexity, penalties for international tax compliance will be addressed in the next chapter.

Chapter Four

International Penalties

With technology and transportation creating a smaller and smaller world, the ability of a taxpayer to have international business transactions or assets has grown substantially. With the IRS interested in the worldwide income of American taxpayers, tax laws were created to fight against hiding income and assets. Of course, the penalties for non-compliance relating to international taxes are substantial.

A book of its own could be written about international penalties. The scope of this book is domestic US taxpayers. This chapter will briefly review penalties for international taxes, but you should know that it can be more complicated than one chapter allows. A qualified professional in international taxes would be your best option.

IRM 20.1.9 is a great resource on penalty abatement for international reporting penalties.[1]

In general, the IRS is allowed to assess penalties called "Assessable Penalties." Assessable penalties are not subject to the normal tax code deficiency procedures. These penalties are required to be paid upon notice and demand without a separate notice requirement before assessment. Some nuances would be that assessable penalties are not taxes, and therefore not subject to a statute of limitations, which is totally different from the normal penalties associated with tax returns. Most penalties are based on a tax due because of noncompliance. But many tax returns for international assets are informational only, meaning there may not be a tax due, only a requirement of the taxpayer to notify the IRS. So, the IRS has in its arsenal the ability to assess a penalty that isn't based on a tax due. That said, international tax compliance is a unique animal regarding how the IRS administers the tax law and subsequently uses penalties to ensure compliance. I.R.C. § 6501(c)(8) often governs the statute of limitations with respect to international information returns.[2]

It's rare that someone doesn't know that they have assets or income. This is particularly so when dealing with international sources. The IRS assumes that if a taxpayer has international tax exposure that they are sophisticated enough in their knowledge to know what constitutes compliance. Furthermore, the IRS also believes that only high income earners hold international assets and park their income beyond the

---

1. Internal Revenue Service, U.S. Dep't of Treasury, Internal Revenue Manual § 20.1.9 (2021), *available at* https://www.irs.gov /irm/part20/irm_20-001-009.

2. I.R.C. § 6501(c)(8) (2022).

eyesight of the IRS, because those high income earners want to keep the IRS blind about their financial life. With that as a background, the IRS maintains that taxpayers who conduct business or transactions offshore or in foreign countries have a responsibility to exercise ordinary business care and prudence in determining their filing obligations and other requirements. The IRS's position is that it is not reasonable or prudent for taxpayers to have no knowledge of, or to solely rely on others for, the tax treatment of international transactions.

The IRS takes a tough stance against excuses, believing that anyone who has assets or income overseas should exercise due diligence and prudence. Their attitude is tough luck if the trustee of a foreign estate refused to turn over information to a US taxpayer. The IRS doesn't care. And even if a reasonable excuse was allowed on the taxpayer's domestic tax return regarding a tax, the IRS may not agree that the excuse existed for the required foreign information return. This also includes a taxpayer's reliance on a foreign return preparer before filing a personal tax return. The bar is set high for reasonable cause to abate that penalty. Because of the high stakes in international tax compliance, the appeals process is different. Normal appeals of penalty abatement are different. Appeals currently provide a prepayment, post assessment appeal process for all international penalties. Appeals also provide for an accelerated process for certain international penalties.

International penalties are assessed on Form 8278 (Assessment and Abatement of Miscellaneous Civil Penalties), with a Form 886-A (Explanation of Items) attached to identify what penalty is being assessed, how the penalty was calculated, and why reasonable cause was not applicable.

Just be aware, a normal tax return has an audit statute of three years, meaning that the IRS has three years to audit it for a tax due. However, the IRS takes the position that I.R.C. § 6501(c)(8) extends the statute for assessment after the foreign tax information has been filed. In other words, even though a taxpayer attaches forms disclosing foreign income and assets, the various attached foreign returns have their own statute of limitations, so that if there's a failure to file a foreign return, then the statute of limitations never starts. But once the foreign tax return is filed, then the three-year statute of limitations applies. Thus, failing to file information returns may affect the statute for assessment on the related income tax return.

While I.R.C. § 6501(c)(8) may apply to extend the limitations period for assessment on the related tax return, there is a reasonable cause exception.

There are other penalties available to the IRS for missing tax information from international sources. Just know that when dealing with international tax compliance, the rules are different and not in deference to the taxpayer.

As a side note, reliance on a tax professional can be a winning strategy. In *Kelly v. Commissioner*, the taxpayer created a foreign corporation that required Form 5471 to be filed.[3] Of course, the forms were not timely filed, and the IRS assessed a failure to file penalty. During the trial, the taxpayer stated that he relied on his CPA to advise him on the filing requirements. The Tax Court cited *Neonatology*[4] and found that the taxpayer had shown reasonable cause reliance on a competent tax professional by providing relevant information to him. Even though the CPA was in error in timely filing the Form 5471, the taxpayer was not required to second guess the tax professional. So,

---

3. Kelly v. Comm'r, T.C.M. (RIA) 2021-76 (T.C. 2021).

4. Neonatology Associates, P.A. v. Comm'r, 115 T.C. 43 (T.C. 2000).

there is hope for reasonable cause when reporting foreign returns. But check with a tax professional who specializes in this area.

Chapter Five

Grounds for Abatement

In the previous chapters, you were exposed to the various types of penalties. Now, the real work begins in determining how, if possible, those penalties can be removed. As stated before, the IRS has been tasked to administer the tax law, with some parts of the law explicitly written, while other parts of the law leave it to IRS discretion. When talking about penalty abatement, it's important to understand what penalty was assessed; it's from there you can determine what remedies are available.

There are four main ways for the IRS to abate penalties,[1] with a fifth option for appeals:

    1. Reasonable Cause

---

1. Internal Revenue Service, U.S. Dep't of Treasury, Internal Revenue Manual § 20.1.1.3 (2020), *available at* https://www.irs.gov/irm/part20/irm_20-001-001r.

2. Administrative Waivers

3. Statutory Exceptions

4. Correction of IRS Error

5. Hazards of Litigation

Reasonable Cause

The first remedy for penalty abatement is "Reasonable Cause." This phrase is important because it is written directly into tax law as a valid excuse to remove penalties. Because this phrase is written in tax law, the IRS and taxpayers sometimes fight in court over what is reasonable. Although IRS has leeway in how it is interpreted, the courts sometimes step in to apply its definition. For example, in I.R.C. § 6651 for failure to file or pay tax, the statute explicitly states that the penalty will be assessed "unless it is shown that such failure is due to reasonable cause and not due to willful neglect."

It is most important when discussing reasonable cause that you know exactly which penalty you are trying to abate. It matters; because the prism of reasonable cause for an accuracy penalty will be different than a failure to file. So, when you are reading regulations, IRM, or tax court opinions, ask yourself what penalty is being discussed.

So, to start, what is "reasonable cause"? Unfortunately, the IRS doesn't provide a checklist. Instead, they claim it is based on "all the facts and circumstances," which is a legalese way of saying, "we'll know it when we see it." However, you can use some well-known cases as a reference: death, significant illness, unforeseen absences, or even things like fires, calamities, and other occurrences you may see in an action film. To show reasonable cause, you will have to show that your client was subject to extenuating circumstances directly contributing to non-compliance.

Reasonable cause has been interpreted to require the taxpayer to establish that either it exercised ordinary business care and prudence but was, nevertheless, unable to comply or that undue hardship would have resulted from compliance. As a forewarning, the courts do not agree on what reasonable cause means in various circumstances. It is a mixed bag. Therefore, a similar set of facts can be interpreted both ways, even in the court system. The bottom line is that you can't lose by requesting penalty abatement when there's isn't a clear answer from the court system and be prepared to rebut the IRS when they bring up another court case that supports their position.

In a landmark tax case, *United States v. Boyle*, the Supreme Court set forth a bright-line rule for the enforcement of tax regulations and explained that to qualify for a refund of penalties, "the taxpayer bears the heavy burden of proving both (1) that the failure did not result from 'willful neglect,' and (2) that the failure was 'due to reasonable cause.'"[2]

Although the term "reasonable cause" is not defined in the Code, Treasury Regulations require the taxpayer to demonstrate that he exercised "ordinary business care and prudence" but nevertheless was "unable to file the return within the prescribed time."[3]

For failure to pay, the regulation further elaborates that a taxpayer's failure will be excused for reasonable cause where:

---

2. United States v. Boyle, 469 U.S. 241, 245 (1985).

3. *Boyle*, 469 U.S. at 246 (quoting Treas. Reg. 301.6651-1(c)(1) (as amended in 1973)).

"the taxpayer has made a satisfactory showing that he exercised ordinary business care and prudence in providing for payment of his tax liability and was nevertheless unable to pay the tax or would suffer an undue hardship . . . if he paid on the due date."[4]

Accordingly, "reasonable cause" can be shown if the following factors are met: the taxpayer exercises "ordinary care," and (1) the taxpayer was nevertheless "unable to comply" with tax obligations, or (2) the taxpayer would have suffered an "undue hardship" by paying the tax.

The Courts consider "all of the facts and circumstances of the taxpayer's financial situation" to determine if the taxpayer exercised ordinary business care and prudence.[5] In addition, consideration is given about the nature of the tax that wasn't paid.[6]

The phrase "willful neglect" is not defined or discussed in the Code or congressional committee reports. The Supreme Court stated that it "may be read as meaning a conscious, intentional failure or reckless indifference."[7] The Court also stated that "it would be logical to assume

---

4. Treas. Reg. 301.6651-1(c)(1) (as amended in 2004).

5. Treas. Reg. § 301.6651-1(c)(1) (as amended in 2004). *See, e.g.,* East Wind Indus., Inc. v. United States, 196 F.3d 499, 507 (3d Cir. 1999).

6. Treas. Reg. § 301.6651-1(c)(2) (as amended in 2004).

7. *Boyle*, 469 U.S. at 245.

that Congress intended 'willful neglect' to replace 'refusal'—both expressions implying intentional failure."[8]

An example of reasonable cause occurred when taxpayers were penalized for filing their 1989 personal income tax return late. In April 1990, their child had heart surgery, when the tax return was due. The taxpayers spent months in the hospital with their child. Unfortunately, their child died in August 1990. Months later, the taxpayers filed their 1989 tax return in October. The IRS believed that the Failure to File penalty was appropriate. The Tax Court disagreed, stating that caring for the ill child was enough reasonable cause in this circumstance.[9]

Like with all interactions with the IRS, documentation is your friend. Without it, you are at the mercy of the government. Many arguments for penalty abatement were lost not because of the facts, but the documentation of those facts. Gather any information that lends credence to your client's story, including medical documents, death certificates, insurance claims, and even photographs. The more relevant documentation, the better. Later in this book, proper documentation and the best practices for referencing it will be discussed.

When throwing down the "reasonable cause" card, the IRS is going to want demonstration or evidence that your client acted "in good faith." That means that they exercised all reasonable business caution and care, which is another fancy way of saying that they made every effort to put things right as soon as possible.

Reasonable cause is not a magic wand that can be waived indiscriminately. To evaluate the penalty abatement, the IRS examines your

---

8. *Id.*

9. Tabbi v. Comm'r, T.C.M. (RIA) 1995-463 (T.C. 1995).

client's tax filing history. Even the most heartfelt sob tale won't suffice if they are serial offenders. The client's story won't be believed. However, if they had been honorable citizens—or, at the very least, decent taxpayers—then the credibility of reasonable cause will be much stronger.

And let's face it, this also involves making your client seem more human. Tax penalties are created from a line that IRS deemed that was crossed. Those penalties are not created from emotion, but human beings are the ones who are responsible for compliance. When representing your client, you should point to the human element of the circumstances that created the penalty.

Proving reasonable cause is part storyteller (honest stories, of course), part strategist, and part number cruncher. It is probably the most used technique for penalty abatement. Your expertise lies in crafting a reasonable cause to match your client's situation and presenting a convincing argument that changes the IRS's opinion about your client. We will now discuss the various excuses or reasonable cause that your client can submit.

Death or Serious Illness

Death or serious illness of the taxpayer or a death or serious illness in his/her immediate family can be the basis of reasonable cause.[10] This could include a spouse, sibling, parent, grandparent, or child. Documentation would include the relationship to the responsible

---

10. Internal Revenue Service, U.S. Dep't of Treasury, Internal Revenue Manual § 20.1.1.3.2.2.1 (2011), *available at* https://www.irs.gov/irm/part20/irm_20-001-001r.

individual and dates of the death or serious illness. Also include why this event caused non-compliance and if other business obligations were hampered in addition to the tax obligations. In the case of a corporation, estate, trust, etc., the death or serious illness must have been of an individual having sole authority to make the deposit or payment or of a member of such individual's immediate family. To add to the mix, document how compliance started soon after the event. Illness or incapacity generally does not prevent a taxpayer from filing returns where the taxpayer is able to continue his business affairs despite the illness or incapacity.[11] The taxpayer won't be able to use his sick child as reasonable cause when he is leaving that care to a private nanny while he earns his high income.

Destruction by Fire or other Casualty

In some cases, natural disasters qualify automatically, like a federal disaster area if it affected the taxpayer's location where records were stored.[12]

Unavoidable Absence

In the case of a corporation, estate, trust, etc., the absence must have been of an individual having sole authority to execute the return or

---

11. Hazel v. Comm'r, T.C.M. (RIA)2008-134 (T.C. 2008); Watts v. Comm'r, T.C.M. (RIA) 1999-416 (T.C. 1999).

12. Internal Revenue Service, U.S. Dep't of Treasury, Internal Revenue Manual § 20.1.1.3.2.2.2 (2020), *available at* https://www.irs.gov/irm/part20/irm_20-001-001r.

make the deposit or payment.[13] Some tax professionals believe that unavoidable absence could also include being in rehab, jail, or held hostage in another country.

Reliance on Tax Professional

In general, reliance on a tax professional could be considered reasonable cause, but it depends on the facts and the type of penalty. When using reliance on a tax professional, court opinions differ particularly regarding tax filings versus tax advice. So, when doing your research, you must ask yourself what penalty abatement is requested. In general, the failure-to-file penalty is a high bar to overcome for abatement. In *Boyle*, which is frequently cited in these matters, the Supreme Court said that filing a tax return was the responsibility of the taxpayer that cannot be delegated as reasonable cause, even if it was the return preparer's fault.[14]

Consistent with that thought, the failure to pay can also be complicated. One district court even stated that failure to pay penalties still applies if the tax adviser embezzled the funds.[15] In one important tax court opinion, the taxpayer's efforts to comply, which included consulting with a tax adviser, were considered key factors in the

13. Internal Revenue Service, U.S. Dep't of Treasury, Internal Revenue Manual § 20.1.1.3.2.2.1 (2011), *available at* https://www.irs.gov/irm/part20/irm_20-001-001r.

14. *Boyle*, 469 U.S. at 245.

15. Kimdun Inc. v. United States, 202 F.Supp.3d 1136 (C.D. Cal. 2016).

penalty abatement.[16] In another tax court ruling, the court noted the compliance history of the taxpayer in weighing the reliance on a tax professional.[17]

So, it really depends. The IRS doesn't like any reliance defense on tax advisers for reasonable cause. They don't believe that it is consistent with ordinary business care and prudence. If bad advice (not related to failure to file or failure to pay) is the central reason for a penalty, the Tax Court established some criteria in *Neonatology Associates, P.A. v. Commissioner.*[18] The Court had a three-prong test: 1) Was the tax professional competent in the tax subject matter; 2) Did the taxpayer provide necessary and accurate information; and 3) Did the taxpayer rely in good faith on the adviser's judgment?

Because it depends on the penalty, more information will be discussed in the upcoming chapters on specific penalties.

Unable to Obtain Records

But what about being unable to get the proper records? Surely, this is a reasonable cause! The IRS has a subsection in the IRM about the

---

16. Neonatology Associates, P.A. v. Comm'r, 115 T.C. 43 (T.C. 2000).

17. Frederick J. Kuckuck v. Comm'r, T.C.M. (RIA) 1993-393 (T.C. 1993).

18. Neonatology Associates, P.A. v. Comm'r, 115 T.C. 43 (T.C. 2000).

inability to get records: IRM 20.1.1.3.2.2.3.[19] It has been argued, "I wanted to comply, but I just couldn't get the records." With that excuse, a successful abatement depends on what penalty you are talking about. Reasonable cause will be acceptable for taxpayers required to make deposits or payments of trust fund taxes only when the taxpayer was unable to have access to his/her own records. In addition, abatement is available if the facts indicate civil disturbances hindered the taxpayer's ability to make deposits or payments. Once again, it is up to the taxpayer to prove that the taxpayer was hindered and tried unsuccessfully in getting the business records. The mere fact that the taxpayer was incarcerated, or his books and records were seized by the IRS doesn't rise to the level of reasonable cause.[20]

When evaluating requests that cite the inability to obtain records as the reason for failing to timely comply, the IRS will consider the following:

1. Why the records are needed to comply;

2. Why the records were unavailable and what steps were taken to secure the records;

3. When and how the taxpayer became aware that they did not have the necessary records;

---

19. Internal Revenue Service, U.S. Dep't of Treasury, Internal Revenue Manual § 20.1.1.3.2.2.3 (2009), *available at* https://www.irs.gov/irm/part20/irm_20-001-001r.

20. Labato v. Comm'r, T.C.M. (RIA) 2001-243 (T.C. 2001); Young v. Comm'r, T.C.M. (P-H) 1989-480 (T.C. 1989), *aff'd* 937 F.2d 609 (6th Cir. 1991) (unpublished).

4. If other means were explored to secure the needed information;

5. Why the taxpayer did not estimate the information;

6. If the taxpayer contacted the IRS for instructions on what to do about the missing information;

7. If the taxpayer promptly complied once the missing information was received; and

8. Supporting documents such as copies of letters and responses reviewed in an effort to get the needed information.

Mistake was Made

An "oops" is not a strategy for penalty abatement, but it can be an add-on for other reasonable cause. Typically, the IRS believes that mistakes are the taxpayer's problem and not a reason for penalty abatement. But if a mistake supports other facts and circumstances, then the IRS reviews the request according to IRM 20.1.1.3.2.2.4:[21]

1. When and how the mistake was known

2. What was done to correct the mistake.

3. The relationship between the taxpayer and person who made the mistake if it was delegated.

---

21. Internal Revenue Service, U.S. Dep't of Treasury, Internal Revenue Manual § 20.1.1.3.2.2.4 (2009), *available at* https://www.irs.gov/irm/part20/irm_20-001-001r.

4. If timely steps were taken to correct the mistake

5. Supporting documentation.

Delegated to Someone Else

This is one of the most common reasonable cause requests, because many times taxpayers delegate their tax compliance responsibilities to another person. And that delegation can come back to bite the taxpayer later when the delegatee fails to perform. In *Boyle*, the court's opinion was clear that the filing of a tax return is a personal non-delegable duty of the taxpayer.[22] Consistent with this court case, the Court of Federal Claims stated that delegating the filing of payroll tax forms and making those deposits to an employee was not reasonable cause when the employee didn't know how to use the tax software.[23] While the taxpayer can choose to delegate as a matter of business practice, it doesn't relieve the taxpayer of the obligation. The fact that a return was not filed when due because of the oversight or forgetfulness of the taxpayer or of an employee of the taxpayer generally (though not always) has been rejected as reasonable cause for not imposing the delinquency penalty.

---

22. *Boyle*, 469 U.S. at 245.

23. All Stacked Up Masonry, Inc. v. United States, 150 Fed. Cl. 540 (Fed. Cl. 2020).

Employee Embezzlement

When employees are negligent or commit malfeasance, the IRS doesn't consider it reasonable cause in general.[24] This is consistent with the denial of reasonable cause when there is a lack of oversight, which allowed the malfeasance. The rule seems to be that the company is entitled to reasonable cause only where it can show it was incapacitated.[25] This incapacitated state is similar to an inability to pay due to hardship. However, blaming an employee for embezzlement doesn't constitute reasonable cause for penalty abatement for failing to pay. There are plenty of court cases where lack of oversight, which includes not finding employee embezzlement until it is too late, doesn't qualify. For penalty abatement to have some merit, the company needs to show that the embezzlement caused undue hardship in failing to pay timely.[26]

Lack of Necessary Return Information

What about "I just didn't have all the necessary information to prepare an accurate return?" The courts have held that the "unavailability of information or records does not necessarily establish reasonable cause

---

24. Conklin Bros. of Santa Rosa, Inc. v. United States, 986 F.2d 315 (9th Cir. 1993); Howe Now, Inc., 85 A.F.T.R.2d (RIA) 2000-2121 (Bankr. W.D. Ark. 2000).

25. American Biomaterials Corp., 954 F.2d 919 (3d Cir. 1992).

26. Pacific Wallboard & Plaster Co. v. United States, 319 F. Supp. 2d 1187 (D. Or. 2004), aff'd, No. 04-35511 (9th Cir. 2005).

for failure to file timely a tax return."[27]   A taxpayer should timely file with the best estimates or amend the return as permitted by law.[28]

Ignorance and Mistakes

Ignorance of the law can be deemed reasonable cause, but rarely gets approved.[29] The inadvertent mistake of mislaying, and thus failing to timely mail, has been found to be reasonable cause when the taxpayer did all the prudent things except leave it on a table by accident for over a week after the deadline.[30] In one instance, a taxpayer claimed to mail an S-corp tax return, and the court believed that his other actions, such as sending other shareholders, etc. their Form K-1s constituted reasonable cause, even when the IRS claims to have never received the corporate tax return. Commonly, the taxpayer didn't have any proof of the mailing, and the court took that into account in the totality of the actions of the taxpayer.[31]

   Ignorance only goes so far, but it is allowed for items that are ambiguous in nature or unusual occurrences such as being an inex-

---

27. Jacobson v. Comm'r, T.C.M. (RIA) 2003-227 (T.C. 2003).

28. Estate of Vriniotis v. Comm'r, 79 T.C. 298, 311 (T.C. 1982).

29. Internal Revenue Service, U.S. Dep't of Treasury, Internal Revenue Manual § 20.1.1.3.2.2.6 (2011), *available at* https://www.irs.gov/irm/part20/irm_20-001-001r.

30. Willis v. Comm'r, 736 F.2d 134 (4th Cir. 1984).

31. Ensyc Technologies v. Comm'r, T.C. Summ. Op. 2012-55 (T.C. 2012).

perienced trust administrator, which can easily happen for taxpayers suddenly in charge of an entity after someone's death.[32] The key is to show good faith effort in trying to get professional tax advice, and not relying on a TikTok video. This is said in jest, but you understand that taxpayers can't seek and rely on just any advice that they receive. The source has to be considered one of quality professional tax advice.

As stated before, the IRS doesn't like mistakes or ignorance of the law, but the IRS does take into account the following criteria in evaluating reasonable cause[33]:

1. When and how the taxpayer became aware of the mistake;

2. The extent to which the taxpayer corrected the mistake;

3. The relationship between the taxpayer and the subordinate (if the taxpayer delegated);

4. If the taxpayer took immediate steps to correct the failure after it was discovered; and

5. The supporting documentation.

---

32. United States v. Northumberland Ins. Co., Ltd., 521 F.Supp. 70 (D.N.J. 1981) (ambiguous law); Vaughn v. United States, 536 F.Supp 498 (W.D. Va. 1982) (inexperienced trustee).

33. Internal Revenue Service, U.S. Dep't of Treasury, Internal Revenue Manual § 20.1.1.3.2.2.4 (2009), *available at* https://www .irs.gov/irm/part20/irm_20-001-001r.

The IRS also takes into consideration the following criteria for claims of ignorance for reasonable cause:[34]

1. The taxpayer's education;

2. If the taxpayer has previously been subject to the tax;

3. If the taxpayer has been penalized before;

4. If there were recent changes in the tax forms or law which a taxpayer could not reasonable be expected to know;

5. The level of complexity of a tax or compliance issue; and

6. If the taxpayer made a reasonable and good faith effort to comply with the law.

Health Problems of Taxpayer or Family

Consistent with death or serious illness previously mentioned, the Tax Court has ruled that reasonable cause can exist when incapacity is due to another family member that is under the care of the taxpayer.[35] This doesn't mean that minor illnesses such as stress will suffice. Examples of serious illness include emergency hospitalization, emotional

---

34. Internal Revenue Service, U.S. Dep't of Treasury, Internal Revenue Manual § 20.1.1.3.2.2.6 (2011), *available at* https://www .irs.gov/irm/part20/irm_20-001-001r.

35. Tabbi v. Comm'r, T.C.M. (RIA) 1995-463 (T.C. 1995).

disability, and mental illness.[36] For these types of health issues, there needs to be documentation that reflects the hardship that cause the lack of compliance. It may be possible to introduce psychiatric studies showing that depression due to a family death lasts for six to twelve months (or whatever period of time best suits the taxpayer) to explain an extended delay between the death and time that the taxpayer came into compliance. I cannot stress enough that you just saying that it happened is not credible. There needs to be supporting documentation such as a medical opinion.

Constitutional or Religious Objections

Taxpayers (often tax protesters) have made frequent arguments that various aspects of the tax system are unconstitutional. When these arguments fail, as they routinely do, the taxpayers argue that no penalty should be imposed because a good-faith argument that the tax system is unconstitutional is reasonable cause. These arguments have likewise failed.[37] In a similar vein, in a losing battle, taxpayers have raised religious objections to the tax system and the duty to file.[38]

---

36. Honey v. Comm'r, T.C.M. (RIA) 1992-551 (T.C. 1992).

37. *See* United States v. Jones, 628 F.2d 402 (5th Cir. 1980); Kirschbaum v. Comm'r, T.C.M. (P-H) 1989-526 (T.C. 1989).

38. See Muste v. Comm'r, 35 T.C. 913 (T.C. 1961), *acq.*, 1961-2 C. B. 3; McCurry v. Comm'r, T.C.M. (P-H) 1988-447 (T.C. 1988).

Just Didn't Care

Of course, if a good faith effort and prudence are necessary to show reasonable cause, the IRS and courts agree that taxpayers cannot use a "don't care" attitude as a viable excuse. As a matter of fact, this carries beyond the taxpayer's own tax return, and can be applied to parents of minors, who are required to file returns.[39]

Personal Problems

There is a high bar for reasonable cause related to personal problems. Excuses like marital problems or going through a divorce don't rise to the level of reasonable cause for not filing a return timely.[40]

Lack of Funds

Lack of funds is an acceptable reasonable cause for failure to pay any tax or make a deposit under the Federal Tax Deposit System only when a taxpayer can demonstrate the lack of funds occurred despite the exercise of ordinary business care and prudence. Remember, the lack of funds is about the penalty for the failure to pay, and not the failure to file. Reasonable cause can be established if the taxpayer exercised ordinary business care and prudence but was nevertheless unable to comply within the prescribed time. It requires proving that the tax-payer exercised ordinary business care and prudence in providing for

---

39. Bassett v. Comm'r, 67 F.3d 29 (2d Cir. 1995).

40. Cayabyab v. Comm'r, T.C.M. (RIA) 2012-89 (T.C. 2012).

payment of his tax liability and was nevertheless either unable to pay the tax or would suffer an undue hardship (as described in Treas. Reg. § 1.6161-1(b)) if he paid on the due date. In determining whether the taxpayer was unable to pay the tax timely, you will have to show all the facts and circumstances of the taxpayer's financial situation.

The penalty abatement will not be granted from a general statement of hardship. Treas. Reg. § 301.6651-1(c)(1) and Treas. Reg. § 1.6161-1(b) both explain that the term "undue hardship" means more than an inconvenience to the taxpayer. It must appear that substantial financial loss (e.g., loss due to the sale of property at a sacrifice price) will result to the taxpayer for making tax payments on time.

The IRS will question if money was spent unnecessarily on a lavish lifestyle, and whether the taxpayer thought that investing in speculative assets and illiquid assets was better than paying taxes on time. In other words, the taxpayer can't put himself in a precarious and speculative position or live a lavish lifestyle only then to claim to have reasonable cause because he is suffering the consequences of his own behavior.

A taxpayer will be considered to have exercised ordinary business care and prudence if he made reasonable efforts to conserve sufficient assets pay his tax liability and nevertheless was unable to pay all or a portion of the tax when it became due. In determining if the taxpayer exercised ordinary business care and prudence in providing for the payment of his tax liability, the IRS considers the type of tax that wasn't paid. Not turning over trust fund taxes withheld from employee paychecks because there weren't enough funds is a higher hurdle to overcome than making estimated payments, because the funds to pay the trust fund taxes should already be available at the time of paying the employees. An example of prudence could be attempts to pay notwithstanding a natural disaster that ruined a business.[41]

The Software Did It

Believe it or not, some taxpayers blame the tax preparation software for their error. One taxpayer failed to report his social security income and had incorrect deductions. The court denied his penalty abatement when he claimed that the software was his tax adviser. Without proof that the software was in error, the courts denied the taxpayer's reasonable cause argument.[42]

It's Reasonable Cause or Not

The IRS has to either accept the reasonable cause or not. There's no middle ground. The 11th Circuit Court of Appeals held that no equitable reduction was allowed for late filing and late payment penalties.[43] Each penalty is fully enforceable unless reasonable cause existed. There's no splitting the baby in half like King Solomon decreed in the Old Testament. The Court found that each penalty is fully

---

41. Custom Stairs & Trim, Ltd., Inc. v. Comm'r, T.C.M. (RIA) 2011-155 (T.C. 2011) (taxpayer cut benefits and payroll and attempted to sell its real property to pay its taxes on time following the impact of Hurricane Ivan.)

42. Powell v Comm'r, T.C.M. (RIA) 2016-111 (T.C. 2016).

43. In re Sanford, 979 F.2d 1511 (11th Cir. 1992).

enforceable unless the taxpayer had reasonable cause, in which case the penalty is to be abated in full.

Administrative Waivers

The IRS has the authority to grant administrative waivers. The first and greatest potential abatement to discuss is the First Time Penalty Abatement (FTA). It does exactly what its name implies. To qualify, the taxpayer must not have the same penalty in the previous three years and be current on their filing and payments. An FTA can be applied multiple times, as long as the taxpayer has a clean record for the previous three years, meaning that an FTA can be applied multiple times during a decade.

Penalties eligible for FTA include:

Failure to File – when the penalty is applied to:

    1. Tax returns – I.R.C. § 6651(a)(1)

    2. Partnership returns – I.R.C. § 6698(a)(1)

    3. S Corporation returns – I.R.C. § 6699(a)(1)

Failure to Pay – when the tax shown on the return is not paid by the due date – I.R.C. § 6651(a)(2)

Failure to Deposit – when the tax was not deposited in the correct amount, within the prescribed time period, and/or in the required manner – I.R.C. § 6656

Taxpayers can receive relief from one or more of these penalties on a tax return during a single tax period. The IRS considers FTA relief regardless of the penalty amount.

How to Qualify for FTA

A taxpayer may qualify for FTA if there is a good history of tax compliance. The IRS considers a good history to include the three years before the tax year you received the penalty. So, three years of good behavior without an incident would qualify if it's related to the same tax form. A taxpayer won't be able to request an FTA if there's no three-year period of consistency.

Example: You request a FTA for a Failure to Pay Penalty on your client's 2022 tax return. If the client doesn't have any unresolved penalties on tax returns for 2019, 2020 and 2021, the FTA will be available.

First Time Abate Relief and Unpaid Tax

The FTA is available even if the tax is not paid in full. A zero balance isn't required to request an FTA. You can request FTA even if the taxpayer hasn't fully paid the tax on the return, which is causing the penalty to incur on a monthly basis. However, the Failure to Pay Penalty will continue to increase (.5% per month) until the tax is paid in full. Here is an IRS example from their website:

> [A taxpayer] didn't fully pay [their] taxes in 2021 and got a notice with the balance due and penalty charges. You call us requesting penalty relief and we give you First Time Abate. We remove the penalty up to the date of your request. However, the penalty will continue to increase since the tax is not fully paid. Six months later you pay the tax in full and contact us

again to request penalty relief under First Time Abate for the same return. We approve First Time Abate relief for the additional penalty amount that accrued until the date the tax was fully paid.[44]

Statutory Exceptions

Statutory exceptions are already included in the tax code and provide an additional path to penalty relief you should take advantage of. What do we mean by "statutory"? These are enshrined exclusions in the law. There are, for instance, exceptions for underpayments brought on by legal changes. Keeping up with some tax law changes is like a long-running soap opera. If your client's underpayment was caused by a recent tax law change, that may be a statutory exception. To some groups of people, further statutory exceptions can be applicable. For instance, military personnel serving in combat zones may qualify for exemption. Additionally, the IRS occasionally issues specific statutory exceptions, usually following severe disasters. Statutory exclusions have the advantage of being clear-cut. Even though these are stated in the law, you will still need to show that your client satisfies the particular requirements for the exception.

44. Internal Revenue Service, Penalty Relief due to First Time Abate or Other Administrative Waiver (Apr. 26, 2024), https://www.irs.gov/payments/penalty-relief-due-to-first-time-abate-or-other-administrative-waiver.

Mailed a Return on Time

If the tax return was mailed on time but a penalty was assessed, then you will have to prove to the IRS that it was mailed in the United States on or before the deadline to file or pay, was addressed correctly, had the proper postage, and was mailed with the US Postal Service or other designated private delivery service.[45] There are times when the personal or business tax return was filed electronically. Proof for this will require an authorized electronic return transmitter and electronic postmark. If the return was timely filed electronically but was rejected by the IRS, it is considered on time if it is resent or mailed within five or 10 days (depending on the facts) of the initial rejection notice.[46]

Federal Disaster Areas and Combat Zones

If a taxpayer is affected by a federal disaster or serving in a combat zone, penalty relief may be available.[47]

Correction of IRS Error

Then, there are instances when the IRS makes a mistake. It happens often. A statutory exemption exists if you can demonstrate that the IRS made a mistake and that your client relied on that inaccurate information.

---

45. I.R.C. § 7502 and 26 CFR § 301.7502-1

46. IRM 3.42.5.14.6 (05-10-2023)

47. I.R.C. §§ 7508, 7508A

Relied on Incorrect Written Advice from the IRS

If the IRS gave incorrect written advice, your response to abate the penalty will be proof that you relied on the incorrect advice, a copy of the penalty letter, a copy of the IRS's written advice, and an explanation of how you relied on that incorrect advice. Any other supporting documents will also be helpful.

Hazards of Litigation

When the IRS thinks the full amount will eventually be impossible to collect, isn't fully winnable, or not worth the effort, they may be ready to settle the penalties. This is a more complex ground for abatement that calls for knowledge of tax law and bargaining strategies. The Appeals Office has the power to negotiate penalties based on hazards of litigation. Interestingly, the revenue agent or revenue officer cannot use this as a basis for their decision. It is reserved for the Appeals Office, which is why I believe that the Appeals Office is an underutilized source to persuade the IRS about penalty abatement.

Summary

So, there you have it - the grounds for penalty abatement. It's a long list of possibilities and a short list of what actually works. The key to abatement is knowing what type of penalty was assessed, what regulations or court rulings are relevant, and gathering the facts that could be used to persuade the IRS to abate it.

Chapter Six

Failure to File / Failure to Pay

M any of the penalties assessed against taxpayers are based on the failure to file or the failure to pay on time. I.R.C. § 6651 states that "reasonable cause" can be a reason for penalty abatement.[1] The IRS has produced guidelines in the IRM and C.F.R. to assist you in determining how and when these penalties can be removed.

Per Treas. Reg. § 301.6651-1, a request for a penalty abatement for a Failure to File and Failure to Pay must be a **written statement containing a declaration that it is made under penalties of perjury.** For a Failure to File penalty, the regulations state that "If the taxpayer exercised ordinary business care and prudence and was nevertheless unable to file the return within the prescribed time, then the delay is due to a reasonable cause."[2]

---

1. I.R.C. § 6651 (2019).

2. Treas. Reg. § 301.6651-1(c)(1) (as amended in 2004).

Both penalties for Failure to File and Failure to Pay (I.R.C. § 6651) have the phrase "unless it is shown that such failure is due to reasonable cause and not due to willful neglect" as part of the law, meaning that reasonable cause is explicitly allowed for penalty abatement. This is consistent with the language within Treas. Reg. § 301.6651-1.

To prove reasonable cause for failure to timely file a return, the taxpayer must show that he exercised ordinary business care and prudence and was nevertheless unable to file the return within the prescribed time.[3] A taxpayer can show that he did not act with "willful neglect" if he can "prove that the late filing did not result from a 'conscious, intentional failure or reckless indifference.'"[4]

There's a slight difference in establishing reasonable cause for Failure to Pay. In the same paragraph as Failure to File, Failure to Pay is mentioned. You can easily miss it in the long paragraph.

> "A failure to pay will be considered to be due to reasonable cause to the extent that the taxpayer has made a satisfactory showing that he exercised ordinary business care and prudence in providing for payment of his tax liability and was nevertheless either unable to pay the tax or would suffer an undue hardship (as

---

3. Crocker v. Commissioner, 92 T.C. 899, 913 (1989); Treas. Reg. § 301.6651-1(c)(1).

4. Niedringhaus v. Commissioner, 99 T.C. 202, 221 (1992) (quoting Boyle, 469 U.S. at 245-46).

described in § 1.6161–1(b) of this chapter) if he paid
on the due date."[5]

There are other areas where the penalty abatement for the Failure to
File exists. Examples of reasonable cause are listed in Policy Statement
3–2 (Reasonable Cause for Late Filing of Return or Failure to Deposit
or Pay Tax When Due), which is also incorporated in IRM 1.2.1.4.2.[6]

> "Any sound reason advanced by a taxpayer as the cause
> for delay in making deposits under the Federal Tax
> Deposit System, or paying tax when due, will be care-
> fully analyzed to determine whether the applicable
> penalty should be asserted."[7]

The statement then goes on to list various things such as death, serious illness, unavoidable absences, destruction by fire or other casualty,
unable to calculate taxes beyond taxpayer's control, civil disturbances,
and lack of funds for making tax payments. Bear in mind that this is
from an IRS policy, which can be consistent or inconsistent with how
tax courts treat these examples.

---

5. Treas. Reg. § 301.6651-1(c)(1) (as amended in 2004).

6. Internal Revenue Service, U.S. Dep't of Treasury, Internal Revenue Manual § 1.2.1.4.2 (1970), *available at* https://www.irs.g
ov/irm/part1/irm_01-002-001.

7. *Id.*

The abatement for Failure to Pay also can include employment taxes, such as the federal income tax, Social Security and Medicare taxes, and the Federal Unemployment tax.

Failure to File Information Returns

Another source of penalties is the failure to file information returns. These returns have no tax liability to assess, such as Form W-2, Form 1099s, or even non-profit organizations such as Form 990s. Reasonable cause is also available for these penalties, but only if willful neglect is not apparent. Reasonable cause can best be articulated when the events were beyond the filer's control. The IRS will require that the filer acted in a responsible manner before and after the failure occurred.

Such examples could be that in the prior years, the filer was never required to file an information return. Or it could be that it was compliant for years, and now the ball was dropped. A few of these details are listed in Treas. Reg. § 301.6724-1.[8] The regulation further describes reasonable cause as events beyond the filer's control such as the unavailability of relevant business records. Those events are a fire or similar casualty, a statutory or regulatory change that affected data processing, or the absence of a key individual that has sole responsibility for filing the return.

Many times, taxpayers subcontract the compliance for information returns. The same reasonable cause standard exists for the subcontractor as if the taxpayer steps in the subcontractor's shoes. This means that if the subcontractor could have the same excuse as the taxpayer,

---

8. Treas. Reg. § 301.6724–1 (as amended in 2023).

then reasonable cause can be used to abate the penalty. The only additional requirement is that the taxpayer gave the proper information to the subcontractor on time.

The key in penalty abatement, especially for failure to file penalties on information returns, is to show that the taxpayer acted in a responsible manner, such as acting like it wanted to file on time, removing the necessary impediments once it happened, and rectifying the problem promptly. IRS considers promptly to be within 30 days of knowing of the problem. Further information is available in Treas. Reg. § 301.6724-1.[9]

Failure to File Partnership Returns

Partnership returns are similar in that those returns don't have a tax due but are information only to place on the partner's tax returns. For partnership returns, the failure to file penalty is based on the number of partners. At the time of this printing, the penalty was $220 per partner.[10]   But for partnerships, there are some additional avenues for penalty abatement. One possibility for penalty relief is outlined in Rev. Proc. 84-35. The requirements are:

1. The partnership must consist of 10 or fewer partners. A husband and wife filing a joint return is considered one partner.

2. The partnership must consist entirely of US resident individuals or the estate of a deceased partner.

---

9. *Id.*

10. I.R.C. § 6698

3. Each partner has filed their individual tax return on time and reported their distributive share of partnership items.

4. Each partner's items of income, deductions, and credits are allocated in the same proportion as all other items of income, deductions, and credits.

5. The partnership has not elected to be subject to the consolidated audit procedures under IRC § 6221 through IRC § 6233.

If true, then the IRS will allow the abatement request. Reasonable cause can also be considered outside this criteria if necessary.

Most tax professionals will see business returns that report no tax due because it flows to the owner. For S-corporations, the failure to file penalty is the same for each shareholder.[11]

The Case of the Elderly Lawyer

Why the IRS fights certain things is beyond understanding. In a 2023 tax court case, an elderly lawyer was juggling closing his law practice while taking care of this ailing wife. During that time, he failed to file and pay tax, which resulted in the IRS assessing penalties for failure to file and failure to pay employment taxes. The lawyer requested reasonable cause and was denied, so the request went to Tax Court.[12] The question before Tax Court was whether the elderly attorney had

---

11. I.R.C. § 6699

12. Tracy v. Comm'r, T.C. Summ. Op. 2023-20 (T.C. 2023).

reasonable cause and didn't have willful neglect as described in I.R.C. § 6651.

The court stated that the 92 year old (at the time of the opinion) did have reasonable cause. He practiced law for 60 years. For approximately two years, he didn't timely file the employment tax forms, while closing down the law practice. He had hearing loss, mobility problems, and heart problems. He delegated more work to his assistant and another attorney. His lack of mobility required someone else to complete domestic duties, such as grocery shopping, laundry, and cooking, while he attended to his ailing wife of 55 years. I think you get the picture here. The IRS decided that it was worth fighting the penalty. While he delegated the tax compliance while winding down the law firm, he was not aware that his assistant didn't fulfill her duties. Once he found out, he filed the missing employment returns and paid the employment taxes. He challenged the IRS on their penalty assessment. Even during the Appeals, the IRS believed that he didn't meet the reasonable cause standard under IRM 20.1.1.3.2.2.1.[13]

The Court agreed with the lawyer that reasonable cause did occur, based on the notion that his failing health and advanced age resulted in his lack of supervision of his assistant. In the opinion, the court stated that:

Notwithstanding petitioner's many difficulties due to his failing health and advanced age, petitioner was diligent in exercising ordinary business care and prudence. He had systems in place to ensure tax compliance. Petitioner's systems had not previously failed him in his

---

13. Internal Revenue Service, U.S. Dep't of Treasury, Internal Revenue Manual § 20.1.1.3.2.2.1 (2011), *available at* https://www.irs.gov/irm/part20/irm_20-001-001r.

approximately 60 years of solo law practice. It was reasonable, and not willfully neglectful, for petitioner to trust his systems' continued reliability. Further, it was not petitioner's reliance on his assistant but his inability to adequately supervise her (due to his failing health and advanced age) that caused his failure to file. Petitioner acted quickly to file the outstanding returns upon discovering he was out of compliance. Had he been able to supervise his assistant properly, petitioner would have ensured that the returns were filed.[14]

Tax Shelters Won't Work

Reliance on a tax professional that is selling tax shelters is highly frowned upon by the IRS.

The courts have taken a similar stance. If it sounds too good to be true, it usually is. In one case, the court denied the taxpayer's argument that it relied on tax professionals when the advice eliminated more than $200 million in capital gains using a partnership.[15] Similarly, it was considered unreasonable to rely on a tax attorney promoting tax shelters as reasonable cause for an accuracy penalty.[16]

---

14. Tracy v. Comm'r, T.C. Summ. Op. 2023-20 (T.C. 2023).

15. Stobie Creek Investments, LLC v. United States, 82 Fed. Cl. 636 (Fed. Cl. 2008), *aff'd*, 608 F.3d 1366 (Fed. Cir. 2010).

16. 106 Ltd. v. Comm'r, 684 F.3d 84 (D.C. Cir. 2012).

Chapter Seven

Failure to Pay Estimated Taxes

The tax system in the United States is a pay as you go system. Under this system the IRS wants periodic payments throughout the year, which they receive through employee wages and estimated payments. Estimated payments may be required for individuals and businesses throughout the year. These are typically paid in four equal installments. Failure to pay these taxes, or underpayment, can result in penalties.

Estimated taxes are used to pay not only income tax, but other taxes such as self-employment tax and alternative minimum tax. If the amount of income tax withheld from wages or other income is not enough, or if a taxpayer has other sources of income, such as interest, dividends, alimony, self-employment income, capital gains, prizes and awards, then estimated payments will be required.

If there's not enough tax withholdings and estimated tax payments to cover the tax liability, a penalty may still be assessed because the IRS wants its money during the year. This penalty is authorized in I.R.C.

§ 6654. A penalty can also occur if the estimated tax payments are late, even if a refund is due when the tax return is filed. Yes, you read that right. If a taxpayer is required to make estimated payments and is later due a refund, the IRS can still penalize the taxpayer for not paying on time. The theory is that a taxpayer must pay in installments. One can only speculate, but my thoughts are that the penalty was created so that taxpayers wouldn't pay only the last quarter of the year, file their return, and then get a refund. The IRS feels cheated that a taxpayer didn't give them the taxes in the first, second, and third quarter. After all, employees have tax withholdings on a weekly, biweekly, or semi-monthly basis; therefore, taxpayers making estimated payments should be likewise required to make theirs on a periodic basis. What the IRS doesn't scrutinize is that they have no idea who is earning these wages during the year, except when the yearly Form W-2 is filed. It doesn't have to make sense, but it is the world we live in.

The penalty is calculated separately for each estimated tax due date. Therefore, a penalty can exist on an earlier due date even if enough tax was paid at a later date to make up the underpayment.

I.R.C. § 6654(e)(3) specifies the general guidelines for waiver of this penalty.[1] The IRS provides some relief for underpayment in certain situations. I.R.C. § 6654(e)(3)(A) states:

> "No addition to tax shall be imposed under subsection (a) with respect to any underpayment to the extent the Secretary determines that by reason of casualty, disaster, or other unusual circumstances the imposition of

---

1. I.R.C. § 6654(e)(3) (2018).

such addition to tax would be against equity and good conscience."

The problem that most taxpayers face is that the United States Congress authorizes the IRS to make its own regulations. This statute language is a prime example of the IRS being allowed to define what the statute means.

In the next paragraph in the tax code, the statute states the penalty can be waived if a taxpayer or their spouse retired in the past two years after reaching age 62, or became disabled, and there was a reasonable cause (and not willful neglect) to underpay or pay the estimated taxes late.

Interestingly, the United States Congress culled out a specific vocation that changes the rules. I.R.C. § 6654(i) requires leniency toward fishermen and farmers.[2] Other rules apply for non-resident aliens in I.R.C. § 6654(j).[3]

For the requirement of estimated tax payments, the United States Congress does distinguish between individuals and trusts or estates. The rules for estimated payments, and therefore what is considered late, apply differently for trusts and estates. I.R.C. § 6654(l) defines when those estimated tax payments are required.[4]

But what happens when a taxpayer has uneven income during the year? Would it be fair for a taxpayer to make equal payments, when there's not enough income during that same period? The short answer

---

2. I.R.C. § 6654(i) (2018).

3. I.R.C. § 6654(j) (2018).

4. I.R.C. § 6654(l) (2018).

is yes. Even if estimated payments are required in equal amounts, if the taxpayer's income is received unevenly, the penalty may be lowered by annualizing the income and making unequal payments. Form 2210 calculates this method.

In general, the penalty underpayment of estimated tax payments may also be waived if:

- The underpayment was due to a casualty, disaster, or other unusual circumstance and it would be inequitable to impose the penalty, or

- The taxpayer retired (after reaching age 62) or became disabled during the tax year for which estimated payments were required to be made or in the preceding tax year, and the underpayment was due to reasonable cause and not willful neglect.

Generally, most taxpayers will avoid this penalty if they owe less than $1,000 in tax after subtracting their withholdings and credits, or if they paid at least 90% of the tax for the current year, or 100% of the tax shown on the return for the prior year, whichever is smaller. As mentioned before, there are special rules for farmers, fishermen, and certain higher income taxpayers.

Estimated Tax Penalty and Reasonable Cause

IRM 20.1.3.2.7.1 is the go-to guide on penalty abatement for estimated tax penalties.[5] It is one of the hardest penalties to be abated because a disaster alone will not be reasonable cause for this penalty abatement. The estimated taxes are due, and the IRS believes that the taxpayer should have set aside funds already to pay the IRS even if a disaster happened, just like a normal person needs to set aside funds for a mortgage payment, utilities, food, etc.

Federally Declared Disaster Area

The penalty for underpayment of estimated tax generally is not waived as a result of disaster; it has to be a designated disaster area. However, in the case of a federally declared disaster area, a significant fire, or a terroristic or military action "the Secretary may specify a period of up to one year that may be disregarded" in determining whether estimated tax payments were paid on time.[6] In these cases, the IRS will issue a memo with specific instructions regarding the payment of estimated tax in the affected area.

A federally declared disaster area can be reasonable cause if the Secretary of the Treasury determines that an area was affected. The IRS will publish guidelines about how the IRS will administer the tax

---

5. Internal Revenue Service, U.S. Dep't of Treasury, Internal Revenue Manual § 20.1.3.2.7.1 (2011), *available at* https://www.irs.gov/irm/part20/irm_20-001-003r.

6. I.R.C. 7508A (2021).

laws for that area. I.R.C. § 7508A(a) provides that the Secretary may specify up to a one-year postponement period.[7] I.R.C. § 7508A(d) provides for a mandatory and automatic 60-day extension.[8]

IRS computer systems automatically identify taxpayers located in the covered disaster area and apply automatic filing and payment relief. The good new is that these guidelines apply to taxpayers who live or died in the area, or where the books and records are located, or where the responsible tax professional is located. It also applies to relief workers affiliated with a recognized government or charitable organization assisting in the relief activities in a covered disaster area.

The IRS does have a hot-line (866-562-5227) specifically for federal disaster penalty abatement.

Coronavirus Disease Pandemic

In IRM 20.1.3.2.7.2.4, there's penalty relief for postponing federal estimated tax payments.[9] The relief is automatic, so there's no need to contact the IRS, but I add this just in case there's a hiccup with you representing a taxpayer where the IRS, for some reason, forgets.

---

7. I.R.C. 7508A(a) (2021).

8. I.R.C. 7508A(d) (2021).

9. Internal Revenue Service, U.S. Dep't of Treasury, Internal Revenue Manual § 20.1.3.2.7.2.4 (2022), *available at* https://www .irs.gov/irm/part20/irm_20-001-003r.

Notice 2020-23 provides relief under I.R.C. § 7508A(a), postponing federal estimated tax payments normally due on April 15, 2020, May 15, 2020, or June 15, 2020 until July 15, 2020.[10]

Bankruptcy

I.R.C. § 6658 prohibits the assertion of the estimated tax penalty on liabilities during the time during which a bankruptcy proceeding is pending against the taxpayer.[11] This prohibition applies when the tax was incurred by the bankruptcy estate and the court finds that the lack of funds cannot pay the administrative expenses.

Erroneous Refund

Sometimes the IRS makes a mistake by issuing refunds and then stating that the payment is due. If the taxpayer claims that an overpayment was refunded in error, the taxpayer may be entitled to have a portion of the penalty abated.[12]

---

10. I.R.S. Notice 2020-23, 2020-18 C.B. 742.

11. I.R.C. § 6658 (1980).

12. Internal Revenue Service, U.S. Dep't of Treasury, Internal Revenue Manual § 20.1.3.2.7.4 (2013), *available at* https://www.irs.gov/irm/part20/irm_20-001-003r.

Other Penalty Abatement Provisions

Within I.R.C. § 6654, which discusses the penalty for underpaying estimated taxes, there are penalty waivers that are in favor of the taxpayer. The waiver provisions of I.R.C. § 6654(e)(3)(A) are not equivalent to reasonable cause. While reasonable cause may be a basis for penalty abatement for many penalties, it doesn't provide a basis for estimated tax penalties. Once again, it needs to be said: penalty abatement for estimated tax penalties is difficult to win, but there is hope.

I.R.C. § 6654(e)(3)(A) allows the Treasury Secretary to create waivers that are based on discretion in cases that would be against equity and good conscience.[13] Of course, the Treasury Secretary can create its own rules to enforce this statute. To help IRS employees make these decisions, the IRS created IRM 20.1.3.3.2.1.2.[14] Within this IRM section are many points that are reasonable cause for other penalties. Examples include when the taxpayer's records are destroyed by a fire, flood, or natural disaster. Serious illness or injury also is a legitimate basis to grant a waiver. However, the waiver may not be granted based on reliance on a tax professional or lack of funds that could have been reasonably foreseeable.

Requests for a waiver of the estimated tax penalty under I.R.C. § 6654(e)(3)(A) must be submitted in writing and signed by the taxpayer. Waivers may not be granted based on in a phone call. Waiver of the penalty must be specifically approved by a supervisor. And finally, a

---

13. I.R.C. § 6654(e)(3)(A) (2018).

14. Internal Revenue Service, U.S. Dep't of Treasury, Internal Revenue Manual § 20.1.3.3.2.1.2 (2020), *available at* https://www .irs.gov/irm/part20/irm_20-001-003r.

waiver can be granted if a taxpayer retired after reaching 62 or became disabled in the taxable year in which estimated payments were required to be made, or in the preceding taxable year.[15]

IRM 20.1.3 has many other sections regarding penalty abatement for estimated payment penalties, including for corporations, estates, trusts, and foreign corporations.[16] This chapter is not all encompassing of every possible penalty abatement for estimated tax payments. Review IRM 20.1.3 for more details if your client's circumstances are equivalent.

---

15. I.R.C. § 6654(e)(3)(B) (2018).

16. Internal Revenue Service, U.S. Dep't of Treasury, Internal Revenue Manual § 20.1.3 (2022), *available at* https://www.irs.gov /irm/part20/irm_20-001-003r.

Chapter Eight

Accuracy-
Related Penalties

W hen a taxpayer or return preparer isn't paying attention to the tax laws and the tax due becomes substantial, the IRS has the ability to assess accuracy-related penalties. IRM 20.1.5 discusses the assessment and abatement of these types of penalties. As expected, the IRS creates regulations for how these penalties will be enforced. Treas. Reg. § 1.6664-4 and IRM 20.1.5 are great resources regarding these penalties.[1]

The term negligence includes failure to make a reasonable attempt to comply with the rules. The term "disregard" includes any careless, reckless, or intentional disregard of the rules, including those found

---

1. Treas. Reg. 1.6664-4 (as amended in 2003); Internal Revenue Service, U.S. Dep't of Treasury, Internal Revenue Manual § 20 .1.5 (2021), *available at* https://www.irs.gov/irm/part20/irm_ 20-001-005.

in the Code, temporary and final regulations, and revenue rulings and notices.[2]

Treas. Reg. § 1.6664-4 goes into a lot of detail regarding various circumstances surrounding accuracy penalties. Penalty abatement for accuracy-related penalties requires reasonable cause and "good faith." The abatement is approved on a case-by-case basis, taking into account the totality of the circumstances. The taxpayer must show an effort to report the proper tax liability. Such effort can by based on an honest misunderstanding of fact or law, which can include the taxpayer's experience, knowledge, and education. However, a reliance on a tax professional is not carte blanche for penalty abatement. The advice from a tax professional must appear to be competent and reasonable. In other words, stating that the taxpayer relied on just a random person on the street won't be acceptable. Another example of good faith is if an inaccurate information return was relied on by the taxpayer. For example, a Form W-2 was given to the taxpayer, but it contained an error that a reasonable person wouldn't catch. If a taxpayer relied on this incorrect document, then the accuracy penalty could be abated. The same thought process applies to an appraisal value of property. An appraisal by itself doesn't qualify as reasonable cause and good faith. The appraisal must pass the "sniff test" to meet reasonableness, using the correct methodology for the appraisal. Because the taxpayer is required to act in good faith, using other professionals helps, but it doesn't necessarily give all taxpayers an easy excuse for penalty abatement, if the professional's opinion is unreasonable.

For example, taxpayer A hires tax professional B for advice on deducting certain business expenses. B tells A that the deductions are al-

---

2. Treas. Reg. § 1.6662-3(b) (as amended in 2003).

lowed. Taxpayer A has shown good faith if the deduction is questioned by the IRS. However, if taxpayer A seeks advice from a TikTok video on the same deduction, the IRS most likely won't abate the penalty.

Another example is when taxpayer A sells $200,000 in stock during the year. Taxpayer A receives a Form 1099-B showing brokerage sales of stock totaling $180,000, in error, which taxpayer A reports on his tax return. Because of this error, taxpayer A would be allowed to have an accuracy-related penalty abated.

However, if taxpayer A waits until the last day to prepare his tax return, and then files it haphazardly because of his procrastination, the accuracy-related penalty on his return most likely won't qualify for abatement because of his lack of good faith.

When using the reliance on a professional's advice as a basis for the penalty abatement, common sense by the taxpayer must prevail. The IRS will ask if the taxpayer knew or reasonably should have known that the professional was knowledgeable in their area of expertise. In other words, don't use a car dealership's appraisal on a piece of real estate; instead use a competent realtor. The burden of proof for a taxpayer's good faith is on the taxpayer. The taxpayer cannot make unreasonable assumptions or blame a professional's advice that should have been known by the taxpayer to be unreasonable. Once again, the totality of the circumstances, the education and knowledge of the professional, and the reasonableness of the claim are key to showing good faith and reasonable cause to abate accuracy-related penalties. Hopefully, the taxpayer gave all the pertinent data to their professional to render an opinion. The IRS and Tax Court want to know that quality information was given to a quality professional. Absent evidence, the IRS will win. In one example, a taxpayer didn't articulate the reasonable cause to the court because the taxpayer didn't show in court the information that he sent to his accountant.[3] As with many court opinions, the taxpayer lost to the IRS not because of the facts, but because the taxpayer didn't provide facts for the courts to consider.

---

3. Kim v. Comm'r, 679 F.3d 623 (7th Cir. 2012).

Chapter Nine

Tax Return Preparer Penalties

There are times when tax return preparers get penalized for understating a taxpayer's liability by taking an unreasonable position or having a reckless or intentional disregard for the rules and regulations. If the IRS audits a return preparer on their work product, it can determine if the return preparer acted unreasonably in their position. The return preparer can be penalized in violation of I.R.C. § 6694 for understating a tax liability because of their actions.[1] There is an abatement available for reasonable cause relating to an unreasonable position. However, if the act was willful or reckless, there's no reasonable cause remedy available. If the courts determine that the position held by the taxpayer does not cause an understatement

---

1. I.R.C. § 6694 (2015).

of liability, then the return preparer's penalty will be abated. More information is available in Treas. Reg. § 1.6694-2(e)(1) through (6) and IRM 20.1.6.[2]

There are other penalties in I.R.C. § 6695 that can be assessed on return preparers, but can also be removed for reasonable cause. Each of the following penalties are $50 per failure, not exceeding a total of $25,000:

1. Failure to furnish copy to taxpayer

2. Failure to sign return

3. Failure to furnish identifying number

4. Failure to retain copy or list

5. Failure to file correct information returns

For a small tax preparation business, these penalties can be devastating. Also, based on I.R.C. § 6695(f), the IRS can penalize a return preparer for negotiating a refund check. Negotiating a refund check is also a violation of Circular 230 regulations.[3]

Interestingly, reasonable cause is not allowed for I.R.C. § 6695(g) on a failure to be diligent in determining eligibility for certain tax benefits. This penalty happens frequently when a return preparer fails to exercise due diligence in completing the forms for qualification of

---

2. Treas. Reg. 1.6694–2(e)(1) through (6) (as amended in 2009); Internal Revenue Service, U.S. Dep't of Treasury, Internal Revenue Manual § 20.1.6 (2024), *available at* https://www.irs.gov /irm/part20/irm_20-001-006.

3. Treas. Circular 230, 31 C.F.R. § 10.31 (2014).

child tax credits, Earned Income Tax Credit, and Head of Household status. The IRS requires these forms to be completed so that a proper determination of the eligibility can be found. When a return preparer ignores these mandates, then the IRS can assess a penalty on the return preparer.

Sometimes, a return preparer forgets to sign the tax return. If that happens, then Policy Statement 3-5 can apply, which states that a delinquency penalty will not be generally assessed if the tax return was filed timely.[4]

Just so you know, an unsigned tax return is not considered a valid tax return. The IRS won't accept unsigned tax returns for processing. The IRS will return unsigned income tax returns to taxpayers, requesting that the taxpayers sign the tax returns and resubmit them for processing.

---

4. Internal Revenue Service, U.S. Dep't of Treasury, Internal Revenue Manual § 1.2.1.4.5 (2011), *available at* https://www.irs.g ov/irm/part1/irm_01-002-001.

Chapter Ten

Important Documentation

If you've ever constructed a house of cards, you know the need for a strong foundation. Regarding penalty relief, your case is only as strong as the supporting paperwork. This chapter is about building that firm foundation for your argument for penalty abatement.

From writing a simple love note to writing a book, your audience must be considered. The recipient of your cheeky and sappy love note has certain tastes, so does the IRS. Know your audience; the IRS is no different. To them, your client is a number: just another taxpayer complaining about the tax system. They have no emotional interest in the taxpayer nor do they have the patience to read about their problems. A reviewer of your abatement request isn't a therapist or someone who will be impressed with the length of your letter. What they are interested is in documentation. Having an excuse without documentation is a recipe for dismissing your penalty abatement request. What they are looking for is the Goldilocks approach: not too little and not too much, but just right. Your documentation shouldn't be a Post-it Note, nor should it be so voluminous that it is shipped in a box. When creating your documentation for penalty abatement, content is king. Tell your story, prove your story, but keep it short.

Common documents include medical records, bank statements, and correspondence, but it is not limited to that either. Don't assume that the IRS has any records or is organized. They aren't going to do your research for you. The operations at the IRS are very fragmented, to the point that even departments within the IRS don't have access to the same information, and they also have different lingo. It's not uncommon for one department to not understand what the other department is saying, just because the acronyms, lingo, policies, and procedures are different.

Let's talk about medical records. Because medical problems are a common excuse, proving a medical problem is paramount. A stack of medical records isn't what the IRS is really interested in documentation. They don't have medical degrees, can't spell the medical terms, and for sure don't have the experience to determine what is a medical problem that causes tax noncompliance. Really the only documentation you need is a doctor's note that explains that the taxpayer was incapacitated for a certain time period. Going into the type of surgery, the type of medication, the side effects of the experimental drug, or other medical terms and procedures isn't really necessary. Of course, a summary sheet of a hospital stay or similar will add to the doctor's note, but don't feel the need to prove the medical condition beyond a medical professional's note.

Police reports are also a good source. If there's a car accident, identity theft, or other law enforcement assistance that is part of your reasonable cause, a police report of the incident will suffice. One IRS employee told me that sometimes car accidents are used as reasonable cause, but many times only a picture of a damaged car is used as proof.

It has never worked, especially when it's been cut from a magazine picture. The proper documentation would be an accident report with some link to the taxpayer, such as being the driver or passenger.

Similar documentation can be used for floods and fires that destroyed records. Insurance claims or reports of assistance by the fire department will suffice.

Bank statements are also a good source of documents. When gathering bank documents, keep it within the time period that you are trying to get the penalty abatement. Show the complete bank statement that covers the time period. If needed, attach a copy of the signature card to show lack of access to bank information.

Correspondence is another great piece of documentation. Correspondence from the IRS, tax advisors, or other related parties should be added. Assume that the IRS doesn't have a copy of the correspondence that is at issue, because they don't. Many of these IRS letters are computer generated, which means that a form letter with information on it is merged from various computer systems to mail to the taxpayer. The IRS doesn't print and mail a notice, then keep it in a filing cabinet. So that IRS notice that the taxpayer received most likely is the only document of its type in existence. Submitting a copy of that document showing the problem you are trying to solve is the starting point of the penalty abatement. Emails or other letters from a tax advisor or other parties relevant to the penalty abatement should also be kept.

The same goes for tax returns that were submitted to the IRS. The person reading the penalty abatement request doesn't have immediate access to that tax return. As a matter of fact, the IRS computer system doesn't keep record of every line item on that tax return. When a paper return is submitted, it is hand typed into the IRS computer system, but not every line is important, only pertinent lines. So that tax return probably has more information than what the IRS computer system has.

Proof of Hardship

Bank statements can show proof of hardship if that qualifies for penalty abatement in your situation.

Financial records are similarly crucial. That severance letter and unemployment claim become important evidence if your client lost their job. Bank statements that reveal negative balances or unexpected withdrawals may also support your argument. It all comes down to creating a convincing picture that your client is in a difficult situation.

No Originals, Only Copies

Never include the originals of any papers that support your argument; just include copies. Tax returns, bills, medical records, and anything supporting your claims are acceptable. To make it simple for the IRS to understand your reasoning, properly organize these documents and consider making a table of contents or index. You are making things as simple as you can for them to accept.

Chapter Eleven

IRS Abatement Procedures

Initiating the Process

B efore you start the abatement process, you need to have four things already completed:

1. You know the penalty and I.R.C. section that allows the penalty.

2. You have read the penalty statute, IRM section, and regulation that covers the penalty abatement.

3. You have crafted a persuasive argument for your position.

4. You have documentation to prove your argument.

Once you have these things covered, you are ahead of almost all tax professionals. A little bit of time and research on the possible abatement will greatly increase your chances of being successful. Frankly, you will probably know more than the IRS employee reviewing your case when it comes to the federal statute, IRS policies, and tax court rulings.

Taxpayer Entitled to Relief

According to IRM 20.1.1.3.5.2, the IRS employee should waive or abate the applicable penalties if the taxpayer provided an ample explanation.[1] Every penalty abatement stands on its own merits, so the IRS may agree for one penalty but not agree for the other. Once the decision is made, the IRS employee is to document the basis for their opinion. In the interest of fairness, the IRS will consider requests for penalty relief received from third parties, including requests from representatives without an authorized power of attorney. While information may be accepted, no taxpayer information will be discussed with a third party unless a valid power of attorney or other acceptable authorization is secured in writing from the taxpayer. [2]

---

1. Internal Revenue Service, U.S. Dep't of Treasury, Internal Revenue Manual § 20.1.1.3.5.2 (2020), *available at* https://www.irs.gov/irm/part20/irm_20-001-001r.

2. Internal Revenue Service, U.S. Dep't of Treasury, Internal Revenue Manual § 20.1.1.3.1 (2023), *available at* https://www.irs.gov/irm/part20/irm_20-001-001r.

IRS Evaluating Penalty Relief Requests

The IRM has guidelines for IRS employees in evaluating penalty abatement.[3] It's important to understand how the IRS evaluates each request. As a tax professional you should know what and how they are thinking. If you know how the opposition thinks, then you can create a penalty abatement narrative to ensure a higher success rate. When the IRS receives a penalty abatement request, the burden of proof is on the taxpayer, of course. Questions that IRS employees will ask themselves are the parties involved, the taxpayer's ordinary business care and prudence, if other penalty relief applies, and if the obligation to meet the requirement is ongoing.

The IRS will also want to know the penalty or penalties for which relief is requested, with each abatement standing on its own merits. The IRS is not interested in a guessing game about which penalty you are requesting. If it appears to be all penalties, then the IRS will address it appropriately. But if it addresses only one penalty, then the IRS will limit its analysis to what the taxpayer requested. The IRS will also do a mental timeline so that the reasonable cause coincides with the actions that caused the penalty. They will also check previous years to see if your client has an ongoing problem with compliance. If an FTA is available, the IRS will give relief under the FTA guidelines.[4]

---

3. Internal Revenue Service, U.S. Dep't of Treasury, Internal Revenue Manual § 20.1.1.3.5 (2020), *available at* https://www.irs.gov/irm/part20/irm_20-001-001r.

4. Internal Revenue Service, U.S. Dep't of Treasury, Internal Revenue Manual § 20.1.1.3.3.2.1 (2023), *available at* https://www.irs.gov/irm/part20/irm_20-001-001r.

When you start to craft your story, begin with the end in mind: Appeals. Assume that you will lose on the initial request and that all the pertinent facts and documentation will be reviewed by an Appeals Officer. What you don't want to do is start adding documentation only if there's a denial of the penalty abatement. Send the best you have on the front end. Be aware: a perfect reasonable argument for penalty abatement could be denied because the employee wasn't interested. For an IRS employee, denying a request is easy. Don't be discouraged if your argument was reasonable; it may have just dropped in the wrong hands at the time.

There are two main ways to initiate the process: over the phone or via paper. Depending on the circumstances, one choice will be better than the other. For most of the time, requesting a penalty abatement by paper is better than by phone.

Abatement by Phone

The IRS does allow penalty abatement over the phone. If you choose to call, there will be a toll-free number at the top right corner of the notice. The problem is 1) good luck trying to get someone on the phone, 2) good luck getting someone who is qualified and competent to understand what you are requesting, 3) good luck getting an employee who is authorized to abate the penalty, because the dollar threshold on what can be abated isn't public knowledge (but it's believed to be $500 to $1,000 per period), and 4) good luck not getting a courtesy disconnect while you are on the phone. The bottom line is that as a tax professional you can spend hours on the phone with very little to show for it with these types of variables.

If you are going to use the phone, prepare well. You should still have a clear game plan, even if you need to write it down. Be aware of the penalties you're talking about, your arguments for why they should be eliminated, and the supporting data. In fact, write it all down because you'll need to have access to it when you make that call.

While on the phone call, be kind and professional when speaking with an IRS employee. Remember, they're only carrying out their duties. They don't care frankly about how your day went, what you ate for lunch, your previous experience with the customer service of the IRS, etc. When you do get in touch with an IRS employee, they more than likely will be new, as in less than a year. They most likely don't have a firm grasp of the IRM, penalty abatement procedures, tax knowledge, or accounting knowledge. They are trained very little and are asked to sink or swim in dealing with the public on some of the basic problems that taxpayers encounter. More than likely, they can't file their own personal tax returns.

Introduce yourself, your credentials (e.g., are you an attorney, CPA, or enrolled agent), and your reason for the call. The IRS isn't known for chit chat over the phone, so keep it brief and professional. Some people think that asking about the IRS employee's life is a gateway to getting their request granted; that is so far from the truth. The truth is you are only a number in the many phone calls that they will receive that day. As a best practice, always say thank you for their help during a lull in the conversation. They rarely get thanked because most people who call the IRS are not happy.

When you do call, there are some documents that you need at your fingertips:

1. The notice that was sent to the taxpayer

2. The penalty you want abated

3. The reasons why you think it should be removed

4. The facts and explanation that caused the penalty, including what happened and why it happened

5. How the situation prevented compliance

6. What attempts were made to get into compliance once the event was over

7. Supporting documentation such as hospital bills, doctor's notes, receipts, etc.

8. A signed copy of the Form 2848, Power of Attorney with you in case you need to reference it or fax it to the employee. The IRS should already have the POA in their system, but you should have a copy just in case it is needed.

As you can see, there are a lot of variables that need to be considered, including the potential for documentation. Because of the limited authority and expertise of the IRS employee on the phone, making phone calls appears to be the lesser option. Of course, some people have good experiences, but most do not.

Reasonable Cause Assistant (RCA)

To help IRS employees evaluate reasonable cause for penalty abatement, the IRS has question-and-answer software that they use. In another chapter, you will learn about the Reasonable Cause Assistant (RCA). RCA is a computer program that creates a road map for IRS employees to consider penalty abatement. The biggest hurdle with RCA is that it is dependent on the quality of the IRS employee answering the question and the quality of the answer given. Unfortunately, if the IRS employee doesn't understand the facts, or the facts don't line up with the software questions, then your case will get denied over the phone. More information about this process is in the next chapter.

Abatement by Paper

For most penalty abatements, writing is better than a phone call because of the lack of proper customer service from the IRS call center and the authorization dollar limits allowed. At least in a letter you have documentation that can be reviewed thoroughly. And if need be, it can also be forwarded to Appeals, so always prepare your penalty abatement request as if you will need to appeal it. If you spend the time gathering evidence, the logical conclusion is to organize it and send it to the IRS.

Complete the Form 843

For most individual and business penalties, you'll need to use Form 843, also known as "Claim for Refund and Request for Abatement." Form 843 is not for abatement of income, estate, or gift taxes. It is usually for penalty relief, but there are various other uses as well. The instructions for the form list all the possible uses. Form 843 can be used for reasonable cause and for erroneous advice furnished to the taxpayer by an IRS employee. If the error is caused by an IRS employee and is in writing, then write "Request for Abatement of Penalty or Addition to Tax Under Section 6404(f)" on the top of the form.

Explain in detail your reasons for filing this claim and show your computations for the abatement. If you attach any additional sheets, include your client's name and SSN, ITIN, or employer identification number (EIN) on it. Also attach appropriate supporting evidence.

Always assume that the package that you send to the IRS is going to get dropped down a stairwell and mixed in with other taxpayer documents. It should be easy for anyone to pick up the documents and organize them back to their original condition. This means using the format "Page X of Y" on the bottom of the pages, labeling the top of the headers, etc.

A taxpayer can file the form or have their representative file it for them. If a tax representative is filing it, a Form 2848 must be attached showing authorization to represent the taxpayer. Please note that the Form 2848 should reflect the tax period, tax, and possible penalty that allows tax representation. The bottom line is that the Form 2848 should encompass the penalty abatement. If you are filing as a legal representative for a decedent whose return you filed, attach to Form 843 a statement that you filed the return and you are still acting as the decedent's representative. If you did not file the decedent's return, attach documents that show evidence of your authority to represent.

Make sure to fill out the form thoroughly, including the tax years in question, your client's identification, and the specific penalty you're contesting. Remember to attach any relevant supporting documentation. The form is very short. It is best to submit a short letter (less than a page and a half), to attach to it along with the proper documentation. Remember that your audience is an IRS employee who reviews many penalty abatement requests on a daily basis. Make it easy and simple. They are not interested in a long story, but will read your short request along with documentation. With attention spans getting smaller and smaller, expect your request to be skimmed, so keep it well organized with headers and subheaders.

When requesting a penalty abatement, remember that a written request is more like a legal brief than a letter. This is your time to thoroughly present your client's case, including the relevant facts, the applicable law, and your arguments methodically. Start with a concise introduction that clearly identifies your client, the penalty you're appealing, and why they should be reduced or removed. The body of your request, where you will expound on your justifications for penalty alleviation, should come next. Your prior research and documentation will be useful in this situation. A common example is when a medical emergency caused your client to experience great financial hardship or unavoidable accounting issues. Whatever the situation, organize your thoughts clearly and summarize each point with specific examples.

Include copies of all pertinent paperwork, such as letters, bank statements, and medical records. Also, remember to cite these documents in your written work. Make it simple for the IRS to understand your reasoning using language like, "As shown in the attached bank statements (Exhibit A), my client experienced a significant loss of income during the period in question." Use the tax code, rules, or earlier decisions to support your position. It's ideal to demonstrate that your client's circumstance is comparable to one in which penalties were successfully reduced. It supports your position and demonstrates that you have done your research.

A best practice is to have another tax professional or a peer review your abatement case to make sure you have covered all your bases. A second pair of eyes can see mistakes and offer insightful criticism. This is something that we can do for a small fee. Similar to a Form 1040 personal income tax return, the Form 843 has a section for the taxpayer and return preparer to sign under penalty of perjury. Typically, the form goes to the service center where your client would have filed a paper return. However, review the form instructions for more specifics. Send the package via certified mail or similar. Never assume that the

IRS will get the mail or acknowledge its receipt. The tracer will show that it was sent and received for IRS purposes.

Questions to Ask Yourself

Here are the top 11 items every penalty abatement for reasonable cause should have:

1. Copy of the penalty notice from the IRS

2. Copy of the client's signed Form 2848 for your representation

3. The penalties and tax years being requested for removal

4. The reason that the penalty was assessed

5. What happened that caused the noncompliance

6. What the taxpayer did when the circumstances stopped

7. Whether there was a reasonable time between the noncompliance and compliance

8. Whether the taxpayer is chronically noncompliant

9. Whether the noncompliance could be anticipated or whether the client was a victim of circumstances

10. Whether the noncompliance was the result of carelessness or a mistake

11. Sufficient documentation to prove your reasonable cause

Filing an Appeal

After you submit your initial request for penalty reduction, the IRS
may reply with a rejection letter. First you need to carefully study that
IRS denial letter. The letter should explain the grounds on which the
IRS denied your request. This is your guide for what to concentrate
on when you submit an appeal. Did they assert that the proof wasn't
strong enough? Or perhaps they didn't agree with how you interpreted a tax law? Your argument can be more effectively tailored if
you know their justifications. To properly appeal, you must prepare
a proper written protest. Similar to the original request, make sure to
clearly state your arguments and provide supporting data for each. You
may also add any new details or supporting materials that were outside
your first request. Keep in mind that the best course is to present more
specific evidence. Your denial letter should include directions for how
to submit your appeal, including where to send it. It is often forwarded
to the IRS Appeals Office, but confirm the details. You typically have
a deadline to complete this, which is frequently 30 days from the date
on the denial letter.

Interest Relief

The IRS charges interest on the tax liability and penalty. When penalties are reduced or removed, the interest associated with that penalty
should be also. Like any other calculation that the IRS computes,
check to ensure that the interest follows along with the penalty abatement.

Chapter Twelve

Reasonable Cause Assistant

As Jack dialed the IRS's phone number, he braced himself for another long wait. His client was facing a significant penalty, and Jack hoped this call would resolve it. Jack tried to ignore the IRS's on-hold music and started thinking about how his client had been going through a tough stretch. His client's former return preparer (and bookkeeper) had a falling out with a business partner over several months that culminated in the return preparer's firm breaking up at the beginning of last October. As a result, the client missed the extended filing date for his returns and was assessed penalties under IRC § 6651(a)(1) for failure to file. The client and his wife were also going through some serious health issues and were struggling to keep his sole proprietorship afloat. Jack felt like if there was ever a case for abating the failure-to-file penalty, this was it.

Jack finally got through to an IRS Contact Representative and requested abatement for the failure to file penalty. He described all the issues that the client had with his return preparer and what a mess that had been. Jack explained how the client had been worried that the return preparer's personal mess was going to spill over onto him. Finally, he mentioned the client's ongoing illness, hoping that would tip the scales in the client's favor. He answered the Contact Representative's questions and was placed on hold for a few minutes. Jack thought about how the wait was the worst part, but reassured himself that this one was a slam dunk. A few minutes later he was shaking his head in disbelief: "Denied, penalty sustained." As Jack prepared himself to call his client with the bad news, he asked himself "How could that be?" He had gotten a similar penalty abated a few weeks ago that wasn't anywhere near as obvious as this one. "What in the world could be wrong with this IRS operator?" Jack wondered silently. Jack didn't know it, but the source of his frustration was actually somewhat obscure software system called the IRS Reasonable Cause Assistant (RCA). Understanding this tool can give the tax pro a crucial advantage in navigating penalty abatement requests.

Introducing the Reasonable Cause Assistant

Penalties are an unpleasant but important part of the U.S. tax system. In the interest of fairness and equitable treatment, the IRS has long recognized that penalty abatement must likewise be unbiased and evenly applied. The ideal at IRS is for taxpayers with similar facts and circumstances to be treated the same. As the IRS has explored Artificial Intelligence and computer-assisted decision-making, it was only natural to attempt to apply the logical functions and automation of computer systems to the process of penalty abatement.

In 1986, the IRS established an Artificial Intelligence laboratory to explore the application of emerging technologies to tax processing.[1] The IRS would then begin testing a prototype Reasonable Cause Expert System in the early 1990s to address inconsistencies in the abatement process.[2] A limited-use system was operational by 1998, which was later expanded into a program integrated with other IRS systems by 2001.[3] This program is called the Reasonable Cause Assistant.

The RCA is described by the IRS as "a decision-support software program designed to help IRS employees determine penalty relief for Individual Master File (IMF) Failure to File (FTF), IMF Failure to Pay (FTP), and Business Master File (BMF) Failure to Deposit (FTD) penalties."[4] Its use is mandated Service-wide for nearly all IRS employees working on penalty-abatement issues. Some of the most common operators of the RCA include telephone Contact Representatives and Revenue Officers. Taxpayer Advocate Service employees also have access to the RCA but cannot abate penalties themselves as their access to the RCA is for advisory purposes only.

The RCA was intended to make the penalty abatement process more consistent, and therefore more equitable. However, the program's implementation has been the subject of ongoing criticism, particularly from the IRS National Taxpayer Advocate. In its 2010

---

1. Internal Revenue Service, *IRS History Timeline*, 2019, p. 30

2. Rick Schreiber, The Tax Adviser, *IRS Artificial Intelligence Projects (Close Encounters Of An AI Kind,* October, 1992

3. National Taxpayer Advocate, *Annual Report To Congress*, 2010, pp. 199-200

4. IRM 13.1.24.6.1.1 (10-31-2022)

Report to Congress, the National Taxpayer Advocate noted that IRS employees using the RCA made correct penalty determinations in less than half of the cases studied.[5]   In each case, the IRS employees believed that they were using the system correctly. The National Taxpayer Advocate attributed this error rate to training and a reluctance by IRS employees to override the system when it makes the wrong recommendation.

Tax pros advocating for penalty abatement need to understand what the RCA is, how it works, and how to best prepare their clients' abatement requests to be processed by a non-human decision tool.

How the RCA Works

Despite its origins in the AI lab, the RCA does not resemble anything like ChatGPT or Microsoft Copilot. The RCA is very much early 21st century technology. The way that it works is not unlike the financial and retirement planning decision tools that were all over the Internet in the early 2000s. The RCA does not "think" like circa-2024 AI does. Rather, it is a rules-based system that uses a series of logical tests to determine which category of reasonable cause to consider, the timing of events that the taxpayer claims caused his or her noncompliance, and whether a reasonable nexus exists between those events and the taxpayer's noncompliance. The RCA passes these inputs through a series of logical filters to determine whether the taxpayer used "ordinary business care" in their efforts to comply with their tax obligations.

---

5. National Taxpayer Advocate, *Annual Report To Congress*, 2010, p. 198

Depending upon the operator's inputs, the RCA arrives at a recommendation to either abate or sustain a penalty.

When our fictional tax pro, Jack, called the IRS about reasonable cause penalty abatement at the beginning of this chapter, the operator who took the call accessed the RCA system. The IRS operator was then guided by the system using a series of menus. These menus prompted the IRS operator to ask the representative for information about what happened. when it happened, where it happened, who was responsible, the nexus between these events, the taxpayer's inability to comply, and what efforts taxpayer did make to attempt to comply. The operator then selected the appropriate categories for reasonable cause abatement based upon the information supplied by the taxpayer's representative. The categories are pre-determined by the IRS programmers and are based upon IRS internal guidance and policy. What happens at this stage is very important for tax pros to understand: the operator will attempt to make the caller's information fit into one of these pre-determined categories which the system will then use to make a penalty abatement determination. (A list of Reasonable Cause categories that IRS employees will consider in this process is in the Appendix at the back of this book. It's also available online as IRM Exhibit 5.1.15-2.)

As part of the abatement decision process, the RCA will check the taxpayer's account to see if the taxpayer has a compliant filing history for the three years preceding the penalty. If an account passes that check, the RCA is programmed to recommend waiving the earliest penalty as a First Time Abatement (FTA). After the FTA check, the RCA will look at the internal timeline of events it has created and determine if a reasonable nexus exists between the events claimed by the taxpayer and his noncompliance. The logical process is not substantially different from the way the abatement process was considered by human operators before the advent of the RCA. While the RCA aims to assist IRS employees, it actually has an outsized influence on the decision-making environment. Understanding this environment is crucial for tax pros preparing abatement requests.

The RCA Decision Environment

The IRS stresses that the RCA is only a decision-making tool to assist the employee. However, the IRS also asserts that "fair and consistent application of penalties requires employees to make a final penalty relief determination consistent with the RCA conclusion" while also acknowledging that it may be necessary to override the RCA in some cases.[6] The reality is that the IRS workplace culture is heavily biased towards deferring to such tools, especially when their use is mandated. In the study referenced earlier by the Taxpayer Advocate, despite the RCA making the wrong penalty determination more than half the time, none of the IRS employees overrode the RCA and every employee in the study believed that they were making legally correct determinations.[7] Furthermore, when RCA operators do believe that the RCA has gotten it wrong, they must provide a written justification for an override. Most types of users must also obtain managerial approval to override. Therefore, it is easy for employees to go along with the RCA's determination and more difficult to contest it. Because of these factors, users may tend to defer to the RCA when making abatement decisions.

---

6. IRM 20.1.1.3.6.10.3 (11-21-2017)

7. National Taxpayer Advocate, *Annual Report To Congress*, 2010, p. 199

Setting Up For Success With the RCA

When applying for reasonable cause abatement, tax pros need to understand that even though they are dealing with a human being at the IRS, that human being is likely mandated to use the RCA to process the request. Therefore, tax pros need to prepare the request with the RCA in mind.

The RCA performs its analysis based upon facts and circumstances describing the taxpayer's exercise of ordinary business care and their inability to successfully comply with their tax obligations. It is important to keep in mind that there are at least two to three human factors between those facts and the RCA system. One is the taxpayer's recollection of and emotional response to the facts. Another is the tax professional's interviewing skills and presentation skills. The third set of factors is the IRS RCA operator's interview skills and interpretation of the facts. Much will depend upon these human factors.

Tax pros should put adequate effort into preparing the request to make it easy for the IRS operator to select the RCA inputs that will result in an abate decision. Whether the request is telephonic or written, tax pros should take care to organize their request in writing before making the actual request. The information that the tax pro gives the IRS employee is what will be used to select the abatement categories that the RCA will use to make a determination. While reasonable cause advocacy is covered more thoroughly in the rest of this book, here we offer some suggestions that relate directly to the presence of the RCA in the IRS's decision-making environment:

Understand the Criteria

The RCA operator will take the facts and circumstances presented by the person making the request and attempt to make them fit one of the categories in the RCA menus. Help the RCA operator out by organizing your request for abatement around the categories listed in the back of this book in Appendix, which is a copy of IRM Exhibit 5. 1.15-2. Analyze your taxpayer's circumstances against those categories and find a category that fits. Use the names of the categories in your request, words like "absence," "bankruptcy," "death," and "casualty." These are some of the categories the RCA will consider, so go ahead and name them in the request. For example: "This request for abatement due to reasonable cause is based upon the taxpayer's absence from his business due to illness."

Be Specific and Detailed

In addition to clearly stating the penalties (type, tax module, etc.) you are requesting abatement for, it is important to provide a detailed explanation of the facts and circumstances that prevented the taxpayer from meeting his or her tax obligations. Each reasonable cause category the RCA operator selects needs to be supported by substantiating information. The Appendix provides a list of Category Issues and Possible Questions in the right-hand column that can be used to substantiate each category. These are the questions the RCA operator will be asking the caller seeking abatement. It is important to know the answers to these questions before making the call or preparing the written request for abatement. A good practice is to go through the questions with the taxpayer after you have identified an applicable category and fully develop those answers.

It is important that the answers show a nexus between the taxpayer's circumstances and his or her inability to successfully comply with their tax obligations. Tax pros should have an explanation for each category ready. For instance, in the case of the Absence category, the caller will need to answer follow-up questions such as:

1. Who was absent?

2. Date(s) of the absence.

3. Reason for absence.

4. How did the absence prevent compliance?

5. Is documentation provided?

Be able to describe how the circumstance affected compliance. This is very important. For example, if the owner was absent from the business during the filing season, be able to explain why this affected the failure to file tax returns. If there was no one else who could do it, explain this. Show how the absence was beyond their control (for example, debilitating illness) and how the absence affected other aspects of the business operations. The point here is to provide the RCA operator a roadmap to a favorable abatement decision.

It is important to include dates and a timeline of events that led to the noncompliance when connecting circumstances to that noncompliance. The RCA has internal guidance for some of these timeframes.[8] For example, a short illness during the filing season will not

---

8. IRM 20.1.1.3.6.5 (2-22-2008)

likely justify failing to file several months later, while a debilitating months-long illness that stretches past the extended October filing deadline might qualify. While the exact internal timeframes that the RCA uses are not available to the public, practitioners should be aware that they exist and strive to develop a timeline for the taxpayer that is reasonable, documented, and gives them the benefit of the doubt.

Regarding the topic of documentation, tax pros should be aware of something called "oral statement authority," which is a dollar limit on what can be abated without documentation. It is programmed into the RCA. The dollar limit applies per penalty and also per tax module. The IRS has redacted these dollar amounts from disclosure, but anecdotal evidence suggests it is as low as $1,000. If the request exceeds this amount, the RCA will display a message that "oral authority is exceeded" and the operator should advise the caller to submit documentation. When possible, tax pros should be prepared with documentation if penalties are significant.

Demonstrate Ordinary Business Care and Prudence

Tax professionals should provide the RCA operator with details that explain the taxpayer's efforts to comply with their tax obligations. While the negative circumstances that prevented the taxpayer's compliance are of prime importance, it is important to highlight any positive efforts the taxpayer made to avoid or mitigate the noncompliance (e.g., consulting a tax professional, attempting to pay on time, etc.).

While not every penalty abatement case will warrant an extensive development of every point discussed here, tax pros should nonetheless be aware of the factors discussed above and ensure that they have provided enough information to the operator to input into the RCA.

One Final Consideration: TAS

One avenue to penalty abatement that should not be overlooked is
the Taxpayer Advocate Service (TAS). If a taxpayer's case meets the
criteria for TAS involvement you may want to consider requesting
their help on the matter. TAS officers have access to the RCA, but they
cannot actually abate penalties. They may, however, recommend the
abatement to the appropriate IRS function by use of a Taxpayer Assistance Order. TAS can be of great help with penalty abatement because
TAS employees are able to use the RCA to determine which categories
will result in abatement. TAS employees may also help determine if a
recommendation to override is appropriate when the RCA renders a
decision to sustain the penalty.[9] This "insider's view" that TAS has
should not be overlooked by the tax pro as it can be a very helpful tool.

Summary

In summary, the RCA has its pros and cons. However, a good tax
professional understands the rules of the game and can use those rules
to their advantage. This chapter is a goldmine of information for you
to use in helping the IRS see it your way for your client's benefit. At the
end of this book, Appendix A is a copy of the RCA decision making
process as copied from IRM Exhibit 5.1.15-2.

---

9. IRM 13.1.24.6.1.3.2 (05-11-2018)

Chapter Thirteen

State Penalty Abatement

E ach state that levies a state income tax has a unique set of regulations governing fines and exemptions. States with tax regulations as complex as the IRS's include California, New York, and Connecticut, and these states are also just as keen to impose fines for errors. Even states like Florida and Washington, which do not have an income tax, can impose fines on corporations for unpaid sales, real estate, and other taxes.

Consider California as an illustration. In the Golden State, if you miss the deadline for submitting a corporation tax return, the penalty will be 5% for the first month and an additional 5% for each subsequent month, up to a maximum penalty of 25%. Theirs are nearly identical to the IRS's guidelines, but California has its own special penalties, such as the "Understatement of Tax Penalty," which carries a 20% fine on the understated amount.

New York comes next. The Empire State has a long list of potential fines, ranging from the famed "Fraud Penalty," which can be as high as twice the tax owed, to "Fixed Dollar Minimum" fines for businesses that fail to declare their income accurately. To avoid certain fines, New York offers a "Voluntary Disclosure Program," where taxpayers can be honest about prior transgressions. You'll want to be aware of options like these when advising clients.

State-level abatement procedures frequently resemble federal abatement procedures. They include well-known terms like "reasonable cause," "administrative waivers," and even certain state-specific "first-time abate" choices. But always double-check the details. What one state may deem a "reasonable cause" may not be acceptable in another.

Finally, let's talk about reciprocity. Because some jurisdictions have agreements to share tax information, if you receive a penalty in one state, you can receive a visit from another.

Varying State Regulations

Consider the example of taxes that are withheld, for instance. Some states closely follow the federal requirements, while others have completely distinct regulations for determining what kinds of income are liable to having taxes withheld from them. While other states don't require taxes to be withheld from gambling wins, certain winnings in Missouri are subject to taxation.

And what about estimated payments? The IRS is very specific about who must make them and when. However, the thresholds and due dates can vary widely at the state level. Suppose your client owes more than $500 in back taxes. In that case, some jurisdictions require you to make quarterly anticipated payments, while other states raise the threshold to $1,000. If the client doesn't hit the target, you'll find that penalties will be assessed.

Be wary of the varying restrictions surrounding sales and use taxes if you assist a commercial customer. Some states calculate their sales tax depending on the location of the vendor, while others calculate it based on the location of the consumer. The origin-based method is used in some states, while the destination-based method is used in others. This can be very complicated for online stores.

Concerning the reduction of fines imposed by the state, you will frequently find that the state provides fewer options than the IRS. Fewer states have regulations for first-time exemptions, and the criteria for what constitutes a reasonable cause can be more specific. However, many provide some type of penalty relief, whether through administrative waivers or legislative exclusions, and it is essential to become familiar with the choices available in each state in which you practice if you wish to benefit from them.

To put things into perspective, state tax codes are like snowflakes: no two are exactly alike. As a tax professional, it is your responsibility to comprehend these complexities when representing your client in penalty abatement in state matters.

Resources for Different States

As a tax professional, you will need to know the state penalty abatement procedures for your client, when needed. This means knowing where to get accurate and timely information. Here are a few recommendations:

1. Google search engine

2. Official state tax website

3. American Institute of Certified Public Accountants (AIC-PA)

4. National Association of Enrolled Agents (NAEA)

These sources can offer state-specific resources and publications to help you better understand tax issues in your area.

Tax preparation software sometimes has state specific topics that can be helpful. One untapped resource are other tax professionals. A good network of fellow laborers in tax compliance is always a positive in your tax resolution practice.

Be aware of legal databases such as LexisNexis and Westlaw; these are extremely useful resources. Through these platforms, you will have access to state statutes, case law, and administrative codes. When dealing with more sophisticated matters that include significant penalties or murky legal areas, having access to these databases can be a lifesaver. However, it may be overkill for less complicated issues.

Chapter Fourteen

Former IRS Employee Interviews

O ne benefit to being former IRS employees is the ability to know other IRS employees who worked in other divisions. Their knowledge and expertise are invaluable when trying to fix complex tax resolution matters. Networking with these experts in their field is immensely valuable.

This chapter is for you to hear directly from these IRS employees, who were reviewing and authorizing penalty abatements. It is one thing to read about the theory of penalty abatement, but it is far more valuable to hear directly from the people who actually made the decisions. In this chapter, three former employees were interviewed and their comments were transcribed, with a few edits for clarity. These answers are directly in their own words and they have great insight on what IRS employees look for in abatement requests. They are willing to share with you their best wisdom so that you too can be successful for your clients.

Herb Cantor

What is your tax resolution experience?

Herb: I've worked at the IRS for 40 years with 6 years as a small business revenue agent, 19 years as an appeals officer, and 15 years as a large case revenue agent. As a revenue agent, I would consider applying a penalty or not. I would determine if there was a complex tax issue, for example, then I would consider not applying the penalty because the taxpayer may have had a good basis or reason to claim a deduction or not report income. As an Appeals Officer, I would determine if the penalty should or shouldn't be removed.

What are some best practices for penalty abatement?

Herb: There are many cases that I saw in appeals in 19 years, almost every case had a penalty. So I would consider various factors such as maybe your compliance history. If that was good, that might help if you had reasonable cause. I would consider either removing or reducing the penalty. If you acted in a responsible manner, if you relied on a CPA, you might have reasonable cause, but there's so many different factors and variables to consider whether to remove or reduce or leave the penalty as is. I dealt with a lot of CPAs and tax attorneys. Once in a while, I dealt with the taxpayer by themselves, and they would, of course, try to make a case for me to remove or reduce the penalty. And I would consider everything they said. I would ask them if they had any reasonable cause for us to remove or reduce the penalty. I would ask them to tell me why the penalty should be removed.

Many people that I dealt with would just say that it's not fair to have the penalty. Some of them would cite tax court cases that were irrelevant to their position. and they wouldn't do much more than that. And I noticed that a lot of Enrolled Agents, CPAs, and tax attorneys really didn't spend much time making their case. They would argue that the taxpayer shouldn't be liable for it. What I would like to see, which is what I do now when representing taxpayers for all different types of penalties, is I prepare a letter to the IRS that addresses all that the IRS is concerned about, because I know what the IRS is thinking and I know how to tell the IRS. I explain why the penalty should not apply and I cite different court cases, different things, wherever I can find them. Sometimes you need to be a little creative, but I put together a detailed letter that indicates why the penalty does not apply. And I do cite the Internal Revenue Code, Treasury regulations, court cases, anything else that I think is pertinent. I do it in a very neat manner and in a nice letter. And I don't write anything that's 20 pages long. I get right to the point, maybe in 2, 3, 4, or 5 pages where the IRS can easily review the letter, so they are happy that I cited everything that I need so that the penalty can be removed.

Unless asked in a thumb drive, I do put everything in a small three ring binder with tab dividers so they can easily look at it. It gets right to the point, so the IRS doesn't spend hours trying to figure out what I'm trying to say. They understand it and that's why I've gotten penalties removed.

What makes a bad abatement request?

Herb: I can give you a couple. I've seen letters from Enrolled Agents and CPAs that say the penalty is not fair and the taxpayer has never had a penalty before, even though that's really irrelevant. That doesn't mean you can't have one this year. But the main one is just a very poor argument that's in maybe two sentences. You need to cite something in your favor if you want get the penalty removed. I've seen fraud penalties where people ask for the penalty removed completely and to which I said, wait a minute, you committed fraud. I mean, you could have been in jail for what you did, but you didn't. But I've also seen cases where the IRS only applied an accuracy 20 percent penalty where they could have easily recommended the 75 percent civil penalty for fraud. So I tell these people that they are lucky that they got away with only a 20 percent penalty. It could have been a lot worse.

I've had a lot of cases and appeals where it was more technical issues where I got the penalty removed. I had a case where a taxpayer claimed to be a model on a Schedule C and she deducted breast implants as a business deduction. Her justification is that she needed to do it to compete with other women in the industry. The IRS proposed the accuracy penalty. So I looked at the case and I thought first of all, this is not a penalty, for different reasons, so I removed the penalty, I gave her a small part of the deduction as a business deduction, and she took the offer. She just basically wanted the penalty removed. So, she was happy. My best advice is that the IRS is not going to be so quick to remove penalties. They will consider it only unless you give them some ammunition to remove the penalty. That's basically it. I mean, it's as simple as that.

Peter Salinger

What is your tax resolution experience?

Peter: I spent a little over 33 years with the IRS. The first couple of years, I was a field revenue officer, where I actually knocked on doors to collect taxes and delinquent tax returns. About five years in, I was promoted to a first line manager and later became a mid level manager, which meant I oversaw about five first line revenue officer managers and about 75 revenue officers. Later I became an appeal settlement officer, basically it's doing collection work and appeals. I did that for about 19 years before retiring.

What is your best advice in penalty abatement?

Peter: Documentation, life in the IRS, as you know, always comes down to documentation. What could you prove? If it's a smaller amount, like a couple hundred dollars on a penalty, I could listen and make a decision, but the larger penalties, I always needed something in writing is what it came down to. Another part is to look up court cases, to where previous taxpayers have had penalties denied and gone to court to fight the penalty. And if they did, look for circumstances that match your circumstances. You have to figure what circuit that you're going to complete your research. Look for cases within that circuit because those tend to hold more weight than ones that are outside of that particular circuit.

What's your experience with RCA?

Peter: The reasonable cause assistant has too many things that can go wrong. If you put in a wrong answer, everything gets blown up. Basically, it gets denied. I like the old fashioned way where I was able to talk through it and get documentation to it as opposed to checking the boxes, yes or no, If the abatement is denied using the RCA, a letter is sent showing that the penalty request was denied and it gives you your appeal rights. Right now, there's two different letters that go out. If you get in with the field revenue office, and they deny your penalty request, they send you out a letter, but you only have 15 days from the date of that letter to request an appeal. Whereas if you get the letter that's issued by the service center, you get 60 days.

Then there's those miscellaneous penalties. When the service center denies those miscellaneous penalties, what they do is they actually, they send you a letter with appeal rights mentioned at the end discussing 30 days to appeal. Ninety percent of the people missed that at the end of the letter. And then they blow their appeal rights. Those miscellaneous penalties are tough, they assess them, and then you have a chance to say that you disagree with them, but a lot of people just miss that. And me as an IRS employee really didn't realize that either until I started dealing with those international returns such as Forms 5471, 5472 penalties on the international taxpayers. A lot of those civil penalties at the end gave you the appeal rights. You know how people read letters sometimes. They read until they get what they want to see and then they don't go through the whole entire letter.

The other thing to mention is that you when you get to Appeals, only Appeals can consider hazards of litigation. As an Appeals Officer, I can take into consideration the chances of losing in court. Sometimes, it's cheaper for the government actually to settle now than it is to wait for the judge to do it.

An important thing too for a Power of Attorney is to read what your client gives you. A lot of times in the OIC program, I would call the POA and ask them if they reviewed what the taxpayer gave them. The POA sometimes would just put a cover letter on incomplete information. When that happens the POA blames the IRS, when it wasn't the IRS at all, but an incomplete request. When submitting a request, attach the documents going in the order of the request. Don't just slap it together and just send it in. Some of the files I saw were just horrendous.

Billy Fauller

What is your tax resolution experience?

Billy: So I was a revenue officer for close to eight years in the IRS. And then from the point that I left the IRS, I've been in private practice helping folks resolve tax issues and help mitigate other tax disputes. Right now, I'm currently the Resolution Training Specialist for Anthem Tax Services. All we handle is typically tax resolution, tax representation cases in terms of helping folks out with issues in front of the IRS. I am also a national speaker. I frequently speak for the American Society of Tax Problem Solvers.

What are your top three penalty abatement tips?

Billy: First, I would make sure is that you are thoroughly documenting those reasons, those circumstances, because that's what the IRS is going to be looking for. Anyone can tell a story, but it's going to be something else altogether when you can back that up with supporting documentation. For example, "I was in the hospital from August the 18th through the 25th, and then I had mitigating medical issues after the fact." It'd be a whole lot different tell of a story for someone who's just explaining that they had these circumstances happen to them, versus the other person who can explain and document their dilemma. Make sure that the request is fully documented and it has supporting substantiating documentation.

Secondly, typically when you're submitting a request for reasonable cause penalty relief, that relief is eligible to be stacked. So if you had a couple of mitigating factors happen to you, I wouldn't suggest just pinning your hat on one. What you want to do is thread the needle and combine multiple different competing factors together. So if you had something for absence or you had something for hardship, anything that you can stack together is beneficial. That can be found in IRM chapter 20.1, which is the Penalty Handbook. I suggest going through, reviewing that. Matching up the facts and circumstances of what happened to the taxpayer at the time they said it happened and trying to stack multiple competing issues together to give your request a fully built out way of getting through and getting across to the IRS.

And as far as number 3 goes, it is not uncommon for the IRS to deny a perfectly fine, perfectly sound request for penalty relief. It happens all the time. Typically, when IRS employees don't know what they're looking at, they'll just have knee jerk reaction, deny it, and move on to the next abatement request. They've got their stack of work to get through, and they don't have a lot of time to sit and review and consider. They may be unfamiliar with some penalty abatement sections. So it happens a lot and is very common. But the best thing I can suggest and recommend with any penalty relief request is if it gets denied always appeal. And I mean, always. Always appeal.

What are the top three things people screw up?

Billy: What makes a good penalty abatement request can make a bad penalty abatement request. So, for what's good, the mirror opposite would be no documentation. You just write up a letter and you say, all right, this happened to me. "Please, I'm begging, I'm pleading, relieve me of these penalties." So number one would be very skimpy, no cites, no references, just a gimme letter. And that's basically what you're writing is, I want penalty relief and give it to me. So, that would be for sure, number one, no documentation. I'm asking for this, I expect you to give it to me.

The second one would be, you're doing yourself a disservice, no matter if you're a practitioner or if you're a taxpayer, by not looking in the penalty relief handbook, IRM Chapter 20.1. I look at the things that the IRS considers meets the criteria for reasonable cause penalty relief. So, you want to make sure that you familiarize yourself with that section because it walks IRS employees through what they should be thinking about, what they should consider what they should take in as a means for penalty relief, and what they should not take in as a means for penalty relief. So it would be really helpful, really beneficial, no matter who you are, practitioner or taxpayer, to familiarize yourself with IRM 20. 1.

My third one would really be to disengage from the process. So you type up your penalty abatement request, you send it in, and you forget about it. You always want to be monitoring your request where it is, how long it's been, because if it's been longer than, say, 6 to 9 months or 5 to 7 months, then you should consider what your next step is going to be. If you've already submitted the abatement request. You've done the work, but then you kick your feet up and you forget about it. But it's not a one and done, because you constantly need to make sure that you're staying on top of the IRS and that means if they are not responding to your request then you're considering getting the taxpayer advocate involved. You should tell the advocate office that you sent this request five to seven months ago and the IRS hasn't responded to it. Request their help and make sure they respond to it, that they get to it.

Chapter Fifteen

Conclusion

Y ou have finally made it to the end. The information is a lot to consider.

Penalty abatement is not taught in colleges, nor is it found in textbooks. It is mainly found in the I.R.C., IRM, and C.F.R. So, if you feel like you need to read some parts over again, don't feel bad. It takes some practice and review to master the subject matter.

We have explored the complex hierarchy of IRS penalties, which range from Failure-to-File and Accuracy-Related Penalties all the way up to the ever-intimidating Fraudulent Failure to File Penalties. We also reviewed the basis for penalty abatement, how the IRS evaluates the abatement criteria, and what you can do to help your client to get the best possible outcome.

As this book ends, there are a few parting thoughts that should be shared. Always remember to keep your requests orderly, because a poorly organized package is the same as having no request at all. But you won't get a penalty abatement if you don't ask. Never be afraid to ask because you never know who will review your request. Penalty abatement is more of an art than a science.

Your documentation should be sensible and easy to follow because it will be the basis for your claim. The IRS won't do your work for you and will only review what you requested. And finally, the world of taxes is continuously evolving. Keeping up with changing regulations and rules is not a discretionary activity but an absolute must. Consistently educate yourself on tax resolution and never stop learning about what the Tax Courts are opining on penalty abatement.

You're more than just a tax professional in financial matters. You could be the difference in your clients' lives by solving their tax problems. Don't get discouraged in fighting the IRS on penalty abatements. Stay with it, and with your newfound knowledge, you will be successful.

Epilogue

P enalty abatement is a learned skill. It requires a special knowledge of tax law, IRS policies, and an understanding on how the IRS thinks. Not all tax professionals are comfortable representing clients in front of the IRS, nor are many experienced in doing it well. If you or your client need assistance, we are here to help. You can book a short conversation with us on our websites:

www.nordlandercpa.com
www.boon.tax

Continuing education and having a community that understands penalty abatement is crucial in becoming a better tax resolution expert. We want to keep you informed about new developments in tax resolution and penalty abatement.

As a bonus, sample letters and examples are available to you at www.nordlandercpa.com/penaltysampleletters so that you can create the best story possible for your clients.

Appendix

Exhibit 5.1.15-2

Identifying Reasonable Cause Categories

These are only guidelines and are not to be used independently for determining reasonable cause.

Category	Category Issues/Possible Questions
Absence Taxpayer claims he or she was unable to comply because of absence, either his or her own or the absence of another person. IRM 20.1.1.3.2.2.1, Death. Serious Illness or Avoidable Absence	Who was absent? Date(s) of the absence Reason for Absence How did the absence prevent compliance? Is documentation provided?
Assessment-Error The penalty(s) should not have been assessed in the first place, or the taxpayer disagrees with the amount of the penalty(s)	What type of assessment error? TP disagrees with penalty computation A payment was missing Payment was refunded in error Not given credit for extension TP mailed return timely
Bankruptcy The taxpayer claims to be in bankruptcy	What documentation is provided to confirm the bankruptcy?
Casualty Fire, Casualty, Natural Disaster, or Other Disturbance-Reasonable Cause	Date(s) of casualty Type of casualty, i.e. Fire Theft Accident In a FEMA declared area? What was destroyed? Is documentation provided?
Death The taxpayer, a relative, or someone affecting the taxpayer's business died.	Date of death? Who died? Is documentation provided?

Category	Category Issues/Possible Questions
IRM 20.1.1.3.2.2.1, Death, Serious Illness and Avoidable Absence.	
Divorce A divorce prevented the taxpayer from complying	Who got divorced? How did the divorce prevent the taxpayer from meeting their obligation?
Elderly Taxpayer The taxpayer did not comply because he or she is elderly or incapacitated.	Has someone taken responsibility for the affairs of the taxpayer? A legal guardian appointed A child or relative Is there documentation?
Extension Any problems associated with an extension	TP forgot to file an extension Extension and/or payment lost in mail Third party did not file extension
Ignorance The taxpayer did not know about, or was unfamiliar with filing requirements, withholding, etc.; the taxpayer was unaware of income or did not know it was taxable. IRM 20.1.1.3.2.2.6 , Ignorance of the Law.	TP claims ignorance of: Didn't understand filing requirements First time under-withholding of tax First time self-employment First time unanticipated income Believed too little income to file Didn't know the due date Not aware of income Not aware income taxable Involves a foreign language or custom
Illness An illness of the Taxpayer or an illness of someone else caused the failure to comply. IRM 20.1.1.3.2.2.1 , Death, Serious Illness and Avoidable Absence.	Did illness stop the TP from taking care of normal financial activities? Who was ill?
Impairment The taxpayer is physically or mentally impaired.	Has someone taken responsibility for the affairs of the TP? What is the extent of TP's impairment?

Category	Category Issues/Possible Questions
IRS Error Taxpayer claims that an IRS error caused the non-compliance IRM 20.1.1.3.4, Correction of Service Error.	What was the nature of the IRS error? Error in an IRS or SSA Publication IRS employee gave incorrect technical advice IRS incorrectly processed TP's return IRS incorrectly processed TP's payment IRS failed to send promised forms What documentation is provided?
Lack of Forms The taxpayer did not have the form or schedule required to file the return.	Did the TP request an extension of time to file?
Mail Problem Taxpayer claims that return or payment was late due to a problem with the mail. IRM 20.1.1.3.2.2 , Ordinary Business Care and Prudence.	What was the nature of the mail problem? Return/payment sent to another taxing agency Return/payment sent to another creditor Return/payment lost in mail Insufficient postage Delayed in mail TP claims error by postal service. Sent timely to Lock Box
Mitigating Circumstance A mitigating circumstance does not refer to an event beyond the control of the taxpayer, but it is an issue mentioned by the taxpayer. Identifying mitigating circumstances helps to produce a better penalty disallowance letter.	What kind of circumstance does the TP describe? Lack of willful intent TP called IRS for advice, but phones were busy Filing requirements are too complex TP's situation is special or unique First time TP received unanticipated income, self-employment income, etc. TP changed jobs, moved, having marital difficulties TP took corrective action TP detected error in first place TP corrected the error

Category	Category Issues/Possible Questions
Other Select this category only if the case does not fit into another category. An abatement in the Other category requires concurrence by manager. IRM 20.1.1.3.2	What does the TP Claim? When did the event preventing compliance begin and end? What is the basis for the TP's claim? What impact did this have on the TP? What documentation is provided? Does the manager agree to the abatement?
Records Unobtainable The taxpayer was unable to obtain or reconstruct records. IRM 20.1.1.3.2.2.3, Reasonable Cause.	What type of records were unobtainable? From whom was the TP unable to obtain records? Why was the TP unable to obtain the records?
Reliance The taxpayer relied on someone else to file or pay, or relied on the advice of someone else. IRM 20.1.1.3.2.2.5 , Erroneous Advice or Reliance.	Who did the TP rely on? What was the nature of the reliance? Person said the TP did not need to file or pay Person handled everything Person failed to send in return or payment Person failed to file extension What documentation is available?
Relocation A move or relocation resulted in the taxpayer's inability to comply.	A relocation will **not** meet reasonable cause penalty relief criteria. Therefore, no questions are asked in this category. The penalty will automatically be sustained.
Signature One or more required signatures were missing from the taxpayer's return.	What is the nature of the signature problem? Joint return unsigned by husband or wife Not signed, but otherwise complete Spouse unwilling to sign return or check
Tax Law Change The taxpayer's failure to comply was directly related to a change in the tax law. An abatement in the Tax Law	Did the TP cite a specific change in the tax law? Would a return and/or payment have been due if no tax law change occurred? When did the TP become aware of the need

Category	Category Issues/Possible Questions
Change category requires the concurrence of a manager.	to file or pay? Does the manager agree this case should be abated?
Unable to Pay The taxpayer lacked the funds to pay or payment would have been a hardship. IRM 20.1.1.3.3.3, Undue Hardship.	An undue hardship must be more than an inconvenience to the taxpayer. Each request must be considered on a case-by-case basis. The mere inability to pay does not ordinarily provide the basis for granting penalty relief. The taxpayer must show that they exercised ordinary business care and prudence in providing for the payment of the tax liability. Information to consider when evaluating a request for penalty relief includes, but is not limited to the following: When did the taxpayer know they could not pay? Why was the taxpayer unable to pay? Did the taxpayer explore other means to secure the necessary funds? What did the taxpayer supply in the way of supporting documentation, such as copies of bank statements? Did the taxpayer pay when the funds became available?
	See Treas. Reg. 1.6161–1(b) and Treas. Reg. 301.6651–1(c)
Category	**Category Issues/Possible Questions**
Absence The taxpayer claims he or she was unable to comply because of an absence, either his or her own absence or the absence or another person	Who was absent? Date(s) of Absence Reason for absence Could someone else make the deposit? Is documentation provided?

Category	Category Issues/Possible Questions
Bankruptcy The taxpayer claims to be in bankruptcy	What documentation is provided to confirm the bankruptcy?
Bookkeeping Error The taxpayer specifically claims some type of bookkeeping error.	A bookkeeping error will **not** meet reasonable cause criteria. Therefore, no questions are asked in this category. The penalty will automatically be sustained.
Casualty The taxpayer claims he or she was unable to comply because of casualty. IRM 20.1.1.3.2.2.2, Fire, Casualty, Natural Disaster, or Other Disturbance-Reasonable Cause.	Date(s) of casualty Type of casualty (Fire, Theft, Accident) In a FEMA declared area What was destroyed? Is documentation provided?
Computer Failure Either the taxpayer's or someone else's computer failed.	Whose computer failed? Date of computer failure. What caused the computer to fail?
Death The taxpayer, a relative, or someone affecting the taxpayer's business died. IRM 20.1.1.3.2.2.1, Death, Serious Illness and Avoidable Absence.	Date of death Who died? Why couldn't someone else make the deposit? Business shut down because of death No one else was authorized Did not trust anyone else Is documentation provided?
Depository Date Discrepancy The taxpayer claims he or she did not get credit for making a timely deposit.	This category does not fall under reasonable cause criteria. Research will be required to consider other procedures, such as possible waivers, to substantiate the taxpayer's claim.

Category	Category Issues/Possible Questions
EFT Avoidance The taxpayer failed to make a required electronic deposit.	Data analysis will be performed to determine if the non-EFT deposit was made during the waiver period(s). Why was the TP unable to make the mandated deposit?
Embezzlement An embezzler took funds that should have been deposited or took actions to conceal the non-filing of returns.	What steps were taken against the embezzler? What documentation is available? Date(s) of embezzlement
Ignorance The taxpayer did not know, or was unfamiliar with deposit requirements in general. IRM 20.1.1.3.2.2.6 , Ignorance of the Law.	TP claims ignorance of: A change in deposit frequency The deposit requirements Same day Fed Wire EFT payment Need for immediate credit item Bank's cut-off time EFTPS cut-off time The laid-back period
Illness An illness of the taxpayer or an illness of someone else caused the failure to comply. IRM 20.1.1.3.2.2.1 , Death, Serious Illness and Unavoidable Absence.	Did illness stop the TP from taking care of normal financial activities? Who was ill? Why couldn't someone else make the deposit?
Impairment The taxpayer is physically or mentally impaired.	Has someone taken responsibility for the affairs of the TP? What is the extent of TP's impairment?
IRS Error Taxpayer claims that an IRS error caused the non-compliance. IRM 20.1.1.3.4, Correction of Service Error.	What was the nature of the IRS error? Error in IRS publication IRS employee gave incorrect technical advice IRS incorrectly processed or coded TP's account Deposit frequency notice (CP 136) was

Category	Category Issues/Possible Questions
	incorrect What documentation is provided?
Lack of Funds Taxpayer did not have sufficient funds to make deposit.	Why didn't the taxpayer have funds for the tax deposit? Used funds to pay other business expenses Funds were frozen by Court Another government agency failed to pay taxpayer
Mitigating Circumstance A mitigating circumstance does not refer to an event beyond the control of the taxpayer, but it is an issue mentioned by the taxpayer. Identifying mitigating circumstances helps to produce a better penalty disallowance letter.	What kind of circumstance does the TP describe? Lack of willful intent Deposit requirements are too complex TP called, but IRS phones were busy Made some kind of data entry or phone entry error TP's situation is special or unique Overlooked making the deposit Some other inadvertent error TP took corrective action TP detected error in first place TP Corrected the error
Records Unobtainable The taxpayer was unable to obtain or reconstruct records. IRM 20.1.1.3.2.2.3, Unable to Obtain Records.	Why was the TP unable to obtain the records? Records lost, unable to recreate
Reliance The taxpayer relied on someone else to make deposit, or relied on the advice of someone else. IRM 20.1.1.3.2.2.5 , Erroneous Advice or Reliance.	Who did the TP rely on? What was the nature of the reliance? Person handled everything Person failed to make or initiate deposit Person gave bad advice about timing of deposit Person erred about due date or amount

Category	Category Issues/Possible Questions
Reporting Agent A failure on the part of the agent (payroll service) or a problem encountered by the agent caused the deposit to be late.	The agent failed to make the deposit on time Agent provided incorrect information to the TP Agent used incorrect figures Used an incorrect deposit method Unaware of the client's deposit requirements
Tax Law Change The taxpayer's failure to comply was directly related to a change in the tax law. An abatement in the Tax Law Change category requires the concurrence of a manager.	Did the TP cite a specific change in the tax law? Is the TP eligible for a waiver? Would the deposit have been correct if not tax change had occurred? Does the manager agree this case should be abated?
Transition A transition or change to the business caused the deposit to be late or incorrect.	What was the nature of the transition? The business was growing too fast A change in accountant/bookkeeper Change in personnel A business move or relocation

Made in the USA
Monee, IL
29 November 2024